THE HUMANISATION OF SOCIALISM

The Humanisation of Socialism
writings of the Budapest school

ANDRAS HEGEDUS
AGNES HELLER
MARIA MARKUS
MIHALY VAJDA

Allison & Busby, London

eh 6 26

CONTENTS

EDITORIAL NOTE

The essays contained in this volume originally appeared in the following Hungarian journals:

Communism and the Family, *Kortars* no. 10, 1970

The Future of Relations between the Sexes, *Kortars* no. 2, 1970

Marx's Theory of Revolution and the Revolution in Everyday Life, *Kritika* no. 4, 1970

Theory and Practice from the Point of View of Human Needs, *Uj Iras* no. 1, 1972

Women and Work: Emancipation at a Dead End, *Kortars* no. 2, 1970

Community and Individuality, *Kortars* no. 12, 1970

Free Time and the Division of Labour, *Kozgazdasagi Szemle* no. 10, 1971

The Main Tendencies of Marxist Sociology in the Socialist Countries, *Kortars* no. 12, 1968

The Choice of Values in the Long-Range Planning of Distribution and Consumption, *Kozgazdasagi Szemle* no. 9, 1969

The Self-Criticism of Socialist Society: a Reality and a Necessity, *Kortars* no. 7, 1967

1

Agnes Heller and Mihaly Vajda

COMMUNISM AND THE FAMILY

Unlike the utopians, Marx did not give a detailed characterisation of the communist society, for in his view it is people themselves who shape human relations by means of human activity and social struggles; to fix the concrete structure of the future in advance would mean that the ideal would have to be confronted with the reality. However, this omission should not lead us to think that Marx did not posit values without the realisation of which the communist society cannot even be conceived. These values reject alienated human and social relations, but they are not mere negations. Marx founded his rejection of the existing social relations on positive value assumptions: the chief goal is not merely the replacement of the existing social forms with new ones, but the establishment of more fully human individuals and social relations. The abolition of private property and the destruction of the alienated collective authority, which are themes which recur in Marx's communism, are a function of these same positive value assumptions. Neither of these is a goal in itself, but both of them are means and processes aimed at bringing about the "humanised" society, since the end of private property and of the state are the basic preconditions for eliminating (a) the fetishisation of human relations into relations among things, (b) the subordination of people to other people (the social division of labour), and (c) the relation of people to other people as mere means. Since some form of social regulation must always exist, this goal can only be realised by elaborating new kinds of human relations, and this in turn clearly presupposes a relatively high level of development of the productive forces.

Our problem is whether the process of total social transfor-

7

mation *spontaneously* fulfils the preconditions which might enable its goal to be realised, that is to say the positive and non-alienated regulation of human relations. Can the types of person necessary for a genuinely free society be created purely by political and economic activity? The communist transformation of the relations of production, and the transformation of the alienated power structures into forms of self-management at local and societal level, can only be carried out if *our conscious revolutionary intentions* are also oriented towards the transformation of everyday life. These factors are mutually determined. The transformation of the relations of production and the dissolution of the relations of domination are inconceivable without the conscious revolutionary re-structuring of everyday life, and vice versa. This problem was laid out by Engels in *Origins of the Family, Private Property and the State*, in which he stated that the abolition of private property and the withering away of the state necessarily go hand in hand with the dissolution of the monogamous family. He argued that in a communist society, the monogamous family would become a married partnership, but he added that because the new forms have still to be elaborated, there was nothing that could be said for sure about this development in advance.

Why do we consider the family to be the organisational centre of everyday life? Human reproduction clearly does not take part only within the family, for a considerable number of our everyday activities do not occur there and are not connected with it. However, it is the family that brings up the new generations and teaches them the kinds of activity which are necessary in everyday life; in fact, this transfer of the activities of everyday life is the most important aspect of education in the family. In addition to this, the family is the "base of operations" for all our everyday activities: we "leave" it, we "return" to it, and it is our living space, our *home*. And last but not least, the family is the source and determination of the most immediate relations between person and person and between man and woman. As Marx wrote in the *Economic and Philosophic Manuscripts of 1844*:

"In this relation, the extent to which the human essence

8

has become nature for man, or to which nature has become the human essence of man, thus appears *sensuously*, reduced to a perceptible *fact*. From this relation one can thus judge the whole stage of man's formation. From the character of this relation follows the extent to which man has become and conceived himself as a *species-being*, as *man*."

There have been suggestions that in communism it is possible to separate the task of rearing the new generations from the permanent context of close relations between men and women, by establishing nurseries organised by the state or by the whole of society, as the basic units for the formation of the new generations. This concept is not only a utopian one, it also indicates the impoverishment of human life in at least one essential respect. First of all it is in opposition to the value assumptions of communism: it would mean that the inner relationships between adults and children, as organic elements of human relations, would be eliminated. Moreover, it points to the introduction of a new division of labour, with a layer of educators being separated off. However, there is a connection between the rejection of this view and the rejection of the converse idea that children must always be brought up within the monogamous bourgeois family.

The bourgeois family

We do not need to examine the history of the bourgeois family here, for we are dealing with communist societies, and from this viewpoint it is sufficient to analyse the function of the bourgeois family and its contemporary crisis. The bourgeois family was initially integrated into the total structure of the bourgeois relations of production and property. The petty bourgeois family, as a productive unit, is one of its main types, although it is declining not only in terms of its importance to the total social production but also in numbers, as C. Wright Mills has shown. The haute bourgeois family is its other main type: this stands outside the organisation of production, though one of its basic tasks is to guarantee the smooth running of

9

capitalist property; this task is carried out by means of educating one or more of the children to manage the factory or the business. The basis of both main types of family is the transfer of private property by means of inheritance.

The original structure of both types of bourgeois family is in transition. Because of the changes in the structure of modern capitalism, the majority of bourgeois families are no longer organised around production, but around consumption, so that even under capitalism the family's economic function is on the decline. Those features which are usually termed "the dissolution of the family" and "the crisis of the family institution" are probably connected with this change in the structure of modern capitalism.

These features are as follows. (a) The end of monogamy in the strict sense of the term. Divorce has been generally accepted *de jure*, or at least *de facto*, though attention has been focused on its socially negative characteristics; this feature has found its most marked expression in Sweden and Denmark, where it has been suggested that marriage as an institution should be abolished in law. (b) The almost complete elimination *de jure* of the man's authority in marriage, and its reduction *de facto*; this is linked with "women's liberation", the gradual extension of the jobs available to women, the achievement of political equality by women, etc. (c) The transformation of the moral norms connected with sexuality; this has improved the condition of women and is linked with the increase in divorce. (d) The virtual disappearance of the extended family, and its reduction to the "nuclear" family.

From the standpoint of the fundamental value of free choice of human association one must regard this process as positive, even if it leads to conflicts which society is incapable of solving even when it tries to eliminate them in an organised way. The financial problems can easily be solved if the society is well off — this problem is not so serious as that which is caused in the lives of many children by divorce. Another basic problem which springs from this disintegration is the existence of loneliness: the nuclear family diminishes the capacity for intense, many-sided relations — and this is in societies where human associations beyond the family are, almost exclusively, merely

10

functional. This is a problem which is additionally serious where old people are left on their own. If old people live with the nuclear family, in many cases they either act as its servant or they are a burden to it, and if they do not live with the family they are left in utter loneliness. The same problem is encountered amongst divorcees, especially women who have children to bring up — a job which clearly makes it difficult for them to enter new relationships.

This disintegration process is expressed and encouraged by sexual revolution, both as a slogan and as a movement, even though its chief aim is to form free human relations. With regard to this aim, the sexual revolution strives for the total dissolution of the bourgeois family. As with all human relations, of course, the free choice of sexual relations and the freedom to keep on choosing them is a basic precondition for the development and universalisation of Individuality. But the sexual revolution restricts the programme of establishing human associations to the free choice of sexual partners: it does not analyse the relationship between sexuality and the other kinds of intense association, especially the relation between adults and children. The sexual revolution does not provide any solution to the question of how the basic units of the new society are to be formed, and it is one-sided even in its restricted analysis of sexual relations. Because it begins with the fact that the historically available kinds of sexual relation are not free, it thinks that promiscuity is better, overlooking the fact that the most long-lasting, intense, and many-sided human relations such as love and friendship originate in the lives of couples. Behind the slogan of sexual revolution, the assumption lurks that the close link between sexual and family ties always entails the repression of "normal" sexuality, and that one must liberate sexuality from its subordination to any other social relation. This is of course revolutionary when compared with the Christian tradition, in which sexuality has been restricted to procreation. The answers to the twin problems of sexuality and the family must be looked for together, but it would be a backward step to look for them in a new kind of bourgeois family.

Apart from its economic function, the basic social function

11

of the bourgeois family is to shape the kind of personality which guarantees that bourgeois society will run without friction. The marxist theory of society assumes an immediate link between the structure of the personality and the totality of social relations, taking it as natural that the transformation of the relations of production and property will create the kind of person who is adequate to the new society. It has not investigated the specific mechanisms which shape character types in accordance with the social conditions, and consequently it has overlooked the kind of family which does not play a fundamental role in the organisation of production, examining the relation between the family and society simply as a moment of production or of the property relations. Marxist investigations into the basic functions of the bourgeois family have been largely stimulated by the experience of fascism; they have revealed that the family's basic role, apart from its changing economic function, is the shaping of the average personality-type necessary for bourgeois society to function. It is the family that creates those aspects of the human personality which adapt people to the conditions of production and the political conditions of society as a whole, and which make these conditions appear as "natural". The first and most representative of the investigations with this orientation was Wilhelm Reich's *Mass Psychology of Fascism*. This idea stands to Reich's credit, even if we disagree with it on certain points. In our opinion, the shaping of the adequate personality-type within the family does not necessarily have to be explained by *naturalistic* Freudian principles; while it is true that sexual repression can participate in the shaping of the bourgeois personality type, one need not resort to the question of sexuality or sexual repression in order to explain the "production" of the normal (understood as the average) personality.

First, we should like to investigate in detail our previous statement that the family is the primary productive unit of the bourgeois personality, and secondly we should like to give a brief overview of the relevant factors in this process.

A basic human personality is shaped and fixed early in infancy, as a result of inborn traits. Let us call this personality the "psychological character". One of the implicit or explicit beliefs of marxism is that the entire human personality can undergo lasting and radical changes throughout its lifespan, but unfortunately this is an inheritance from sensualism. What can and often does change is the moral character, and even this does not change independently of the psychological character (for example, a negative psychological character rules out any radical moral catharsis). The psychological character is thus shaped mainly in the family, which also transfers its basic moral priorities to the child. However, these moral priorities can later be modified by choice — unlike the psychological character, which cannot be modified. The bourgeois family must ensure that the psychological character of the people who grow up in it are adequate to bourgeois society and its demands. Naturally, this need not be carried out consciously: in fact the task is carried out usually even if the dominant family ideology is openly anti-bourgeois. The formation of a moral character which is not integrated into bourgeois society therefore demands hard work on the psychological character, and this is impossible unless there is a high degree of intellectual capacity.

The parents constitute the basic environment for the young child, and its education in the nursery and child-minding centre always refers back to the family. It is "natural" that the child should love his parents above anyone else, for parents "must" be loved and respected — society expects it. Until the child becomes an adult, his deepest emotional links are with his parents, and he must look for his moral ideals in them: the nursery and later the school furnish other moral ideals, but never in relation to everyday life and never with such immediacy as to direct the child's activities (and actually these ideals do not represent relations for the child). If we assume provisionally that there are exceptional cases where both parents set positive moral examples, it still may be the case that the moral and psychological characters of neither parent correspond to the child's specific endowments. This restriction on the child's choice may lead to character deformation in early childhood (as it does, for example, with children of great men who turn out to be failures). If the child takes the psychological and moral character of his parents as his ideal, in spite of his own specific endowments, it may give rise to abnormal inner

13

tension and even to a weak will. However, if he rebels then his rebellion takes irrational forms: he holds his parents responsible for all the damage done to him, even in cases where problems were not caused by them and they were merely incompatible. In situations in which one or both parents have a moral character that is generally negative, but society requires that the child should love precisely these parents (although there are exceptional cases involving openly brutal or criminal parents where society does not require it), we need only point out in such a situation the child becomes completely homeless: he belongs nowhere.

The bourgeois family is authoritarian; it is not a community. In the vast majority of families even today, tradition and the man's social situation make him the authority, independently of the means at his disposal to exercise this authority. There are families where the woman has authority because of her place in society or her strong personality, but this does not alter the fact that the family is authoritarian. Consequently the modern family is inadequate for teaching the child how to live and act in a community. Even if the parents are in complete agreement on everything, their perfectly harmonised life cannot become a model of social conduct, for their unity is exceptional and would, in principle, be impossible in the context of a larger social unit: even the most harmonious relations between parents are incapable of preparing children for democratic social action. And it is only in exceptional cases that this function can be served by means of relations among children themselves. The links of children are always with parents, and their conflicts are usually solved by reference to the parental authority or to immediate parental intervention: thus we cannot speak even of a relatively independent children's community. And the low number of children makes it impossible for them to form a real community; even in exceptional cases where there are many children in the family, they are not the same age and the difference in ages creates a kind of "natural hierarchy". This comes about because the older children frequently become the parents' representatives, and the authoritarian social conduct of children is prepared by this structure. This happens naturally, even in families where the ideology is

14

anti-authoritarian, for the parents can live their own lives if the obedience of their children is a basic value to them: the "good child" is a euphemistic description for the "obedient child". The child has to beg forgiveness for his misdeeds, regardless of whether or not he admits that his parents are in the right, since from his viewpoint rewards and punishments (whether they are fair or not) come from a position of power. The tasks which belong to the division of labour within the family are likewise allocated "naturally", in an authoritarian way.

The instinct for self-preservation becomes in the family a desire to possess, to have. The bourgeois family is based on the community of property, whether or not it is also a unit of production or owns private property that brings in an income. The family's authoritarian structure means that the use of its property depends on the decision of the family authority; this may lead us to a fight over the use of property within the family, and at the same time to defending the material interests of the family against all other families and groups. An internal struggle for material goods does not have to take place; ideological factors can play a successful part here, though it requires a rare and highly developed intellectual level. At the same time, and quite apart from the ideological priorities, in a society which is based on the family structure it is impossible to avoid defending family property against others. For example, even a family which rejects private property in principle cannot agree to the children giving away all their toys and their clothes: at some point, it will have to bring up the argument "this belongs to you". The modern family thus reproduces the proprietary consciousness and the significant "we-consciousness" of natural communities.

At first, the proletarian family was not a bourgeois family. It was not a bourgeois one in Marx's time either, when the proletariat's material conditions prevented it from being able to develop the preconditions for "normal" bourgeois family life. In that period the proletarian family did not have its own home. Adults and children alike worked for and lived off their income, and there was no opportunity for one family provider to become the authority in the family automatically because of his job. Because the working day was twelve to fourteen hours long there was scarcely any opportunity for real ties to develop between children and parents, and the former grew up on the streets. The gradual improvement in the living conditions of the proletariat enabled its family structure to be bourgeoisified, and stimulated the development of the prevailing type of family, the monogamous bourgeois family. Bernstein noted this phenomenon approvingly (everyone had to be raised as a "bourgeois"), and he also noted correctly the connection between this process and the development of reformist currents in the working-class movement. People who live in a bourgeois way do not desire to transform bourgeois society fundamentally but try to reform it, in order to ensure a higher standard of living. In periods of large-scale economic crisis, the proletarian who has grown up in a petty bourgeois family becomes not a revolutionary but a rebel: this sort of person constituted the mass base of fascism, and fascism would never have succeeded had it not been for the petty bourgeois psychology of a part of the working class.

Of course, the negative role of the bourgeois family in shaping the psychological and moral character does not, it seems, depend completely on the family structure. This limitation applies especially to the "proprietary orientation" and to the particularity of the "we-consciousness". In the first place, however, factors appear to exist which cannot be overcome within the given family structure, such as the essentially authoritarian relationship between children and parents or the absence of community in everyday life. The second and crucial point is that there are certain norms of custom and value orientations which have historically become linked to the modern family in such a a way that it seems virtually impossible to eliminate them from the family as it stands. Therefore a revolutionary transformation of the family which is directed towards the negation of these norms of custom and value orientations would seem to hold out more hope.

Revolution, socialism and petty bourgeois consciousness

The marxism of the Second International regarded the total social process and the shaping of the psychological character

16

as being immediately related, and there was a conviction that the transformation of the former leads mechanically to the transformation of the latter. The bolsheviks initially held the opposite conception: thus in the period immediately after the October revolution it seemed natural that fundamental changes would have to take place in the relations between men and women as well as in the basic forms of community life, precisely because the creation of proletarian power and the removal of the ruling classes does not lead automatically to such changes. Fundamental changes took place in legislation concerning the family, and there were major attempts to transform everyday life completely. Experimental communes were started, similar to the one described in Alexandra Kollontai's novel *Red Love*; the most optimistic documentation of this phenomenon from the period is Makarenko's *The Road to Life*, which beautifully depicts the relationships of community life and the formation of the psyche. It has often been noted that part of the reason for the success of this experiment was the fact that the children in Makarenko's community had not originally been brought up within bourgeois families. However, the ideology which began to prevail in the 1930s, and which restored many of the theoretical notions of the Second International, also reintroduced social democratic notions of the family. There were deliberate measures to re-establish and strengthen the bourgeois family, and although they might have felt it instinctively, they were unconscious of the fact that this strengthened the authoritarian character of the whole system. When the other socialist countries came into being, transformation of the family was certainly not on the agenda, and the only concern was with those aspects of the bourgeois family which were immediately linked with society as a whole: the ideal of the family itself remained untouched. The creation of the new human being which is necessary for a new society to be formed was dealt with entirely in terms of the Enlightenment model, as a problem of the *content* of education (the induction of socialist principles and the norms of collective life, the Enlightenment view of the world, moral influences and so on).

There is, however, another conception which has developed in the history of marxist theory, and it currently plays an

17

important role in the leftist movements of Western Europe. According to this conception, the shaping of the new human being is not merely the result of "ideological influence", nor is this aim merely the mechanical result of the transformation of the social structure; rather, it looks at the development of a new psychological character in relation to the democratic transformation of the units of social production. These ideas were elaborated in the most detailed way by Gramsci, but his conception was not independent of the social experience of the period following the October revolution. Of course the democratic transformation of the structure of the shop floor is also a fundamental precondition for communism, but this does not give us an answer to our problem, for the following reasons. (a) The more developed a society is, the later is the stage at which the individual enters production, and therefore young people increasingly start their working life with a fixed psychological and moral character. (b) The more developed a society is, the less time is spent on production; in fact the reduction of working time is one of its goals, since the formation of many-sided relationships in production alone (or rather in the organisation of production) is inconceivable. (c) Even if occupations and skills are freely chosen, it is nevertheless impossible to determine production from the point of view of the individual. Democracy at the point of production can only become free of manipulation if the democratic way of life and norms of activity have already become natural for the individual when he enters production. In bourgeois society the average person accepts authoritarian direction; he does not seek to handle questions which do not relate immediately to his own life, and broadly speaking he can be manipulated. Pure political democracy, too, is evidently useless for shaping people with new psychological characters: even where there are cases of direct democracy, the basic units of the latter cannot be identified with the central point of social life. It is as inconceivable in modern society as it was in the ancient city-state such as Sparta. This problem can only be solved by means of a radical transformation of the family. The criteria which the new family has to meet are (a) that it must be a democratically structured community in which democratic inclinations can be learned

18

early on, (b) that it must ensure many-sided human relationships, including those between adults and children, (c) that it must ensure the development and realisation of Individuality, for which the basic precondition is the free and recurring choice of human associations even in childhood, and (d) that it must remove the conflicts which spring both from monogamy and from the dissolution of monogamy. This is the kind of solution which can be found in the new type of family, and we shall call it the "commune". Marxist communism is not utopian; the ability to realise the social conditions which correspond to its value assumptions is based on tendencies which are already present in existing society. The question of what kind of family is adequate to communist society can be posed in marxist theory only if the context is not some imaginary "ideal" society, but points to the satisfaction of already existing social needs, even if these are not yet present on a mass scale. We have already noted that the bourgeois family is incapable of satisfying many needs which are on the way to becoming universal; but certain positive needs also exist which point to the transformation of the family, and the varied and increasing number of commune experiments clearly indicate these positive needs. If this new kind of need has registered itself only in circles which are free from everyday material problems, this certainly does not signify that such needs do not exist elsewhere, or that a social movement oriented towards their development cannot bring them into the open.

The commune as the family-type in communist society

In the following paragraphs we shall outline our conception of the family structure in communist society. There is no point in elaborating the details, for it is always the case that modes of organisation of the future cannot simply be the realisation of previous plans; and just as there are many different kinds of monogamous family, the collective family or commune will also emerge in many varied ways. In fact the number of variations will probably be larger, since it is a question of assembling a structure which is much more complex than that of the monogamous bourgeois family. This commune is the "successor" to the bourgeois family, and therefore it is not the basic economic

19

or political cell of communist society. The organisation of society as a whole is entirely independent of the commune, which is the organisational centre of collective everyday life. Our commune therefore has nothing in common with Fourier's *phalanstère* or other plans of a similar kind for communes which function as units of production or for communities which are based on sharing a common living-space. Because it functions *only* as a family, the realisation of our commune is not independent of the socio-political conditions nor of the global realisation of communism; it would help to bring about the communist transformation by creating the type of people required for it. Although its immediate function is to solve the conflicts under discussion, the commune furnishes the pre-conditions for communist changes in the economic and political structure so that they are irreversible. This does not signify that the organisation of communes has to "wait" till the start of the communist transformation: on the contrary, the two processes must start together, and if the situation is favourable, it may be possible for the changeover to communes to come before the full process is achieved.

The commune is a *freely chosen community*: its members choose to belong to it, and they are accepted by all the other members of the community. Individuals enter the commune, and each adult member of the families entering it becomes a commune member as an individual. The membership must of course be sufficiently small to ensure that commune affairs can be carried out by means of direct democracy. All the forms of personal individuality must be respected. The necessary conditions for the operation of the commune are as follows. (a) Work is obligatory: all the able-bodied members of the commune must work and participate in the social division of labour. For example, even in the current context, a man with a high income may not support a woman with whom he has a steady relationship within the commune. (b) No one is exempt from the commune's collective tasks. (c) Everyone in the commune must in some way or other be involved with its children's community, whether or not they have "their own" children. Apart from these necessary conditions, the community does not intervene in its members' lives, jobs, free time or human relations.

There will of course be, as in all communities, preferable modes of human conduct, but except in extreme cases moral preferences will not become moral imperatives: in extreme cases, the commune may expel the member concerned. In our conception, the commune has no value priorities concerning sexual relations. So far in civilised societies, the main source of such value priorities has lain in two factors. The first is that of the proprietary consciousness: the woman is the man's private property, or (in a more up-to-date version) the man and the woman are each other's property. The second factor is the need for children to be cared for. Since the commune is based on the rejection of private property relations, the first of these factors consequently no longer holds. As far as the second factor is concerned, the solution is with the commune, which takes care of those children who are born into it or belong to it even if one of their parents chooses a different partner or leaves the commune, which takes care of those children who are born into it or belong to it even if one of their parents chooses a different partner or leaves the commune. The concrete significance of the absence of value priorities towards sexuality in the commune is that within the confines of a single commune both lifelong couple relationships and promiscuity are possible. The commune does not make promiscuity obligatory: this is important, for similar organisations in the recent past have not only chosen promiscuity but have also been built directly on it. However, this is as much of a restriction of the individual's free development as monogamy is.

Under such conditions, the dissolution of couple relationships not only leaves the children's lives undisturbed, it also diminishes the negative side of divorce for adults. It is not a question of reducing the pain of divorce (since this is not caused by the way of life), but of the possibility that when a relationship has ended, the divorced partners can remain in their original community and not be alone. The commune solves the problem of loneliness in cases apart from divorce. People who are unattached can find a commune with married people: given the present family structure partners in marriage can be lonely too, and because of lack of time or spatial separation etc. married people can be deprived of varied and many-sided human rela-

21

tions, even though they would happily associate with others if they could. Of course, old people's loneliness and feeling of being superfluous disappear in the commune. Communal life reduces the extent of human relations which are built merely on custom and routine. In the modern family, people frequently carry on living with each other because they are simply accustomed to it, because they cannot think of anything better, or because they are trying to avoid the problems which divorce would bring: in the commune, these problems disappear. The commune is not a closed entity, preventing the formation of rich human associations beyond it; external associations will develop spontaneously, for the commune is neither a productive unit nor a political one. To the extent that communes abound, it will be natural for membership to fluctuate among them.

The commune will clearly not have any "officially" stated ideology, but equally clearly a community of people who have freely chosen each other will have some kind of common ideological viewpoint, especially since the commune points to the *revolutionary* transformation of life in one very fundamental respect (at least in the present period). Consequently, ideological problems in the commune would probably give rise to internal conflict.

It does not seem possible that housework can be liberated in the foreseeable future; the growth of the service industry is not a solution to this, nor is the modernisation of housework, although this helps. However, it is possible in the framework of the commune to reduce considerably the amount of time spent on running household affairs, even given the present economic and technical conditions — bigger households are much more economical, and suited to the use of machines. This in itself increases the amount of free time, which can in turn be used in radically different ways in the commune. In the monogamous family, parents with young children are tied to the house, but in the commune the "house" itself enables free time to be spent in a diversified way. Even free time "inside the house" should not be limited to consumption but should be active and cultural, and facilitate personal development. The forms taken by this development cannot of course be determined beforehand, but a cultural framework of this kind will

22

probably enable the community to progress. (This can be demonstrated by historical examples, such as the cultural effects of trade-union communities in former working-class movements.) Of course, this progress only takes place if the community does not limit the development of Individuality, which is something that we have posed in principle.

We have already noted that the commune's most fundamental advantage lies in its treatment of children. What we have been discussing so far involves "finished" people, for whom the commune ensures that already existing problems will be solved. However, one of the reasons why the destruction of the bourgeois family is so fundamental is that it removes many of the negative factors which determine the shaping of the psychological character. Before we examine this question it is important to describe the children's community of the commune. Children are not "brought up collectively" in the commune, they belong to a real children's community. Judgement on children's conduct, their entry into the division of labour and the allocation of rewards and punishments, that is to say the regulation of children's relations, is a function of the age level, and it should be a task not for adults but for the children's community. This does not signify that the relations between adults and children should not be close and many-sided; but they are not simply authoritarian, as they are in the bourgeois family. Children should know that they can decide their own fate in many ways; this leads to an early development of democratic propensities, so that children can become full members of the adult community at a comparatively early age. Even where very young children are concerned, where the authoritarian element of relations between adults and children cannot be eliminated, it is of vital importance that every adult and older child in the commune, and not simpy their "biological" parents, should be involved with them in some way or other; in this way, fixed emotional preferences are absent from birth. As they are growing up, the children tend more and more to choose those adults to whom they are more attracted and to whom they feel linked by basic inner associations, and the converse is also true. The adult members of the commune are not necessarily more attracted to "their own" children, and

23

therefore they can choose those children whose temperament, character and intellect are closest or most attractive to them. Neither adults nor children have to love anyone, nor do they have to love anyone "the most": like every other emotion, love too depends on choice. This diminishes the dichotomy between "mine" and "yours" at the emotional level. However, as distinct from the case of children born in the commune, the free choice of emotional associations is an illusion for those members who join the commune with children. Although this may create conflicts for those who have been raised within the old type of family, we should remember here the experiences of people who feel that they could love a child "as their own" if it had been raised in their own milieu. On the other hand, it is often the case that parents cannot face up to their children's faults, because they are afraid that if these faults were laid bare they would be left with nothing at all (this latter is not always the case today, in families where there are a lot of children).

The commune's community clearly has claims on the children's community. The demands made on them are the same, such as the duty to work (or to study) and the obligatory participation in the joint work of the community. Even if the adult community is obliged to appear authoritarian in this situation, it does not do so as "head of the family", since what the adults are demanding is that obligations are carried out which are the same as their own. The children's community not only reduces the emphasis on the dichotomy between "mine" and "yours", it also prevents the proprietary psychology from developing in other areas. In the children's world, as opposed to the adults' world, all personal property is eliminated: there are many existing children's communities which prove how this can be done. The psychological character of children who grow up under such conditions will encourage the democratic way of life, for they will never accept that a situation where they have no decision over their own fate is natural. At the same time, they will not develop the need to oppress other people. One could argue that existing children's communities are notable for the incidence of cruelty: however, these communities are composed of children who are raised in bourgeois families and seek to act

24

out the drive for power which was developed and simultaneously repressed in the family. A more serious objection might be made, that children's communities could prevent the development of Individuality. In order to avoid this, the commune will have to create the preconditions which will enable not only the adults but the children too to follow their own desires and likings once they have fulfilled their commune obligations. Every child should be able to play in the way he wishes, read what he likes and spend his free time as he likes. At the same time, the development of a free Individuality will be greatly encouraged if the children relate to a large number of adults. If the adults have a fundamentally positive moral character, the children have the opportunity to choose their ideal of everyday conduct in those adults whose psychological and moral character is suited to their specific endowments.

Communes which fulfil their social functions will have definite material preconditions. First of all, the commune cannot be closed: every individual must be entitled to leave the commune whenever he or she likes. Secondly, the commune must have the right to expel a member if it is necessary (the preconditions for this must be guaranteed, with society making apartments available for departing members). In addition to this, the normal functioning of the commune demands a definite level of material prosperity: communes based on poverty fall apart, at least under European conditions. However, there is no great amount of wealth required to establish the commune, especially since individual expenses are considerably reduced by common housekeeping, common libraries, collective child-rearing, etc. As long as communes function in the framework of a commodity-producing society, material problems must be carefully arranged so as to create as few conflicts as possible. Since the commune cannot be separated from society as a whole, this problem can only be solved by reducing income differentials: as long as the communist solution to the issue of payment is not carried through, all the commune can do in this sphere is to reproduce the broader problems in itself.

There are other conflicts which can cause change or dissolution in the commune. Because the commune is the organisational centre of everyday life in communist society, the existing non-communist societies can hinder the development of communes and try to have them dissolved. The ideal type of commune which we have described is itself full of conflicts, but they are not the conflicts of a society which is based on possession: they are "truly human" conflicts. But the influence of the existing societies may cause the reproduction of the old conflicts and structures, and one can expect the development within individual communes of a very strong particular identity which may be the cause or effect of competition or even antagonism among them. There are other important problems which may arise as a result of the fact that the individual communes would be likely to comprise people occupying similar positions in the social division of labour, which might produce significant differences in the standards of living between various communes, with the result that cultural differences are preserved.

It would be utopian to think that the commune alone can solve the most fundamental social problems. There can be no separate political or economic transformation which, by itself, is final or which prevents former social structures from being reproduced. Shop-floor democracy, for example, can easily be deformed into manipulated democracy. A separate solution to the problem of the family is no exception: if the commune remains isolated, it will certainly become deformed. One of the basic social tasks of the members of the commune is therefore to help bring about a communist transformation in every social sphere; conversely, structural change oriented towards communism cannot be made irreversible unless there is a revolution in the family. The shaping of the new psychological character can only come about within the revolutionised family: this is the only place for the mass education of individuals who will participate actively in running social affairs, not only at times of great social crisis but "every day".

2
Agnes Heller

THE FUTURE OF RELATIONS BETWEEN THE SEXES

There are several reasons why it is impossible to make prophecies about the future of relationships between the sexes and within the family. The chief reason is because they form an organic unity with the social conditions and therefore cannot be analysed in isolation. We can only approach the problem by asking what kind of sexual and family relationships are to be expected on the basis of some definite set of social relations prevailing at a certain point in the future. Secondly, even on the basis of a conception of the future condition of social relations, it is still difficult to make predictions. More than ever in the past, mankind is today facing several different social alternatives. Which of these alternatives are in fact realised will depend on human decisions, actions and practice: therefore, the question cannot be answered merely by extrapolating from current social trends. So what can we do? If we set out from 'the given conditions and potential of the present society in its economic, political and social dimensions, we can describe the optimal and least desirable variants of social development, and we can predict the probable development in the sexual and family relationships which depend on these optimal and least desirable variants.

This kind of description itself, of course, involves an element of choice. We choose a future for ourselves on the basis of our values and the attitudes we hold in social conflicts (these two things are integrated in practice). The writer of this essay, a marxist, has chosen a communist future for herself, and this implies a definite attitude to the values which mankind has so far developed. In discussing the future of sexual and family relationships, we shall sketch them into the context of a developing communist society, since this is the value system which we have chosen, incorporating the optimal realisation of the potential of our times. This is not to exclude the possibility of a less desirable or even a repugnant solution, nor to exclude this kind of pessimistic possibility from being dealt with in marxist theory and analysis. But it does mean that those solutions which are possible from the perspective of communism will remain our yardstick for judging the future of sexual and family relationships. In what follows we shall deal mainly, for reasons of space, with the optimal possibility.

During the Renaissance there was already a great variety of sexual and moral rules and customs. The rules of sexual morality were cited as a common example of the changing and incidental character of mores during the Age of Enlightenment. Apart from the question of variety, we are concerned with the following questions. First of all, are there, from a certain point in history onwards, certain inherent values amongst the widely varying moral customs which would appear to be constant and which, if so, could be seen as universal human values, i.e. as factors in the development of the "species-being" (Marx) and which point beyond themselves in their positive value content? In addition, what is the general significance and function of sexual mores, and what is it that makes them specific within the complex of moral customs as a whole? The answers to these questions have a far-reaching influence on the concepts which we form about the sexual and family relationships of the future.

Before the development of civilisation, of class societies, sexual customs were more variable than after. There is no room here to analyse the reasons for this. We should simply point out, however, that this apparent richness hides real poverty: in fact it expresses the limitedness of the tribal world. It reflects, not universality but the absence of universality and individuality. Only one of the values concerning sexual relationships which was more or less formulated in primitive societies and was adapted under civilisation is still functioning, and that is the incest taboo. As time passes this norm becomes instinctive: members of the same family

28

do not even desire each other (at least as a social norm). With this norm, mankind has socially regulated and codified its interests as a species. Therefore the first universal, that is to say the first historically permanent value applied to sexual relationships was not merely born as a result of natural selection but also of social purpose: this remains true even if mankind was not fully conscious of what it was doing. This was the beginning of the process known to Marx as "the pushing back of natural limits" in relation to the sex drive; it is a process which, as we shall see, has in this particular sphere been very restricted.

Starting from the development of civilisation (to repeat: historically, this coincides with the birth of class societies), the variability of moral ethics took on new forms in the sphere of contact between the sexes. Thus a certain variability developed between different classes and strata within the same society. At the same time there arose the institution of marriage, based on private property, together with the social inequality between men and women in sexual and family relationships. The influence of private property on sexual and family relationships developed permanent features which can be found in every existing structure of customs; in spite of their persistence, however, they do not represent universal human values, since they are rooted in the process of alienation. Alienation is the discrepancy between human essence and existence: it is the development of mankind's material powers at the expense of the human essence of individuals and that of whole social classes and strata. This is expressed in many ways in the evolution of sexual relationships in different forms and in different historical periods. One of the common permanent features (and this does not only affect family relations) of every alienated social formation is that, under private ownership, life is oriented towards possession. Only that which is in our possession can we regard as being really ours. Thus the desire for possession becomes a basic drive and motive not only in relation to objects but also in relation to people. If a person is my property, he or she cannot belong to anyone else, just like my land, my cattle, my factory or my home. The relation between men and women is

29

likewise permeated by the motive of possession. In order to avoid any misunderstanding, let us be clear that the drive for possession which dominates sexual and family relationships should not be confused with the aspiration prevailing in every love relationship that the person whom I desire, whom I love, should be "mine". The confusion should be avoided, if for no other reason than that the "instinct" for possession is independent of desire and emotion. The man takes his revenge on the wife who is "guilty" of adultery and on her "seducer" even if he never loved and desired her, simply because she is "his". It is a question of "honour" not to be deprived of something that has been one's property, irrespective of whether one needs it or not, and irrespective of one's degree of need for the object or person. Of course, it should be added that wanting to achieve possession is closely interlinked with the desire that the loved or desired person should be one's own. The motivation for possession becomes overwhelming in this relationship too, and it profoundly affects the desire itself. It is a question of male prestige to possess as many women as possible, and this prestige is enhanced if the women concerned are "hard to get"; on the other hand, women's prestige rests on the number and social rank of their admirers.

In class society, generally speaking, human being does not confront human being: someone occupying a certain position in the division of labour confronts someone occupying a different position. People are only equal if their position in the division of labour, i.e. within the social hierarchy, is similar. This is an equality between unequals, for it is not based on equal human values. A real equality is, of course, possible even between people who are similarly positioned in the social scale; in other words, meaningful relations on a basis of equality are possible even under conditions of alienation. But in the vast majority of cases they are possible under such conditions only between members of the same sex, and primarily among male friends. The relationship between people of different sexes is, as we have already noted, by definition unequal. And above all, the woman is judged not on the basis of her own place in the division of labour but on that of her father's or husband's position in it. It is only the nineteenth and twentieth centuries which have brought some change in this sphere, though even so it is not a significant one. Relationships between the sexes have thus been condemned to be relationships between unequal people, and therefore they reflect the alienation of the species-being.

This inequality is clearly present in every aspect of relationships between the sexes. It is reflected in the sexual aspect, since it is only in exceptional periods that the reciprocity of sexual pleasure is explicitly a universal goal. It is evident from the moral point of view, since what is permissible for the man is prohibited for the woman. It can be seen in the intellectual and juridical spheres too: the latter is demonstrated by the different juridical positions of the man and the woman in the famliy. And the subjective aspect of alienation is silent acceptance of this inequality; revolts against it usually break out in periods of general social revolution or as a result of them (during the Renaissance, the Age of Enlightenment, the early Romantic period, utopian socialism, and then with the spread of marxism).

General social alienation extends to sexual relationships in other ways too, particularly through the mediation of the alienation of morality.

Attitudes oriented towards property presuppose a particularist personality, an individual who strives to maintain himself under given conditions, if necessary to the detriment of others; an individual in whom passions oriented towards his own person dominate — envy, jealousy, vanity and egoism; the kind of person who is incapable of seeing himself at a distance or of regarding himself objectively, and who identifies himself uncritically with his own passions and interests. Parallel with the growth of this particularist personality a morality forms whose function is to channel the particularist demands and to subordinate them to the more comprehensive social needs and interests. Moral imperatives do not remain purely external (if they did, they would not be moral). The individual internalises them, takes them over as integral parts of his own system, his internal code, with some people internalising them to a greater extent than others. Conscience, as

31

the "internal judge", is the form in which the "external judge", i.e. public opinion and its moral judgement, manifests itself in the personality.

Obviously moral principles play an exceptionally important part (even in their alienated form) in the process of humanisation in general, and in the humanisation of relationships between the sexes in particular. Similarly, it is obvious that the antagonism between moral rules and the individual's particularist tendencies contributes at least as much to the maintenance of particularism as to his humanisation.

We are dealing here only with sexual relationships. The rules of sexual morality result only in a partial humanisation of the individual, at the same time as maintaining the contradiction between particularist drives and moral rules (which may themselves be particularist). Jealousy, egoism and the desire for possession are not eliminated: they are simply channelled into areas where they do not conflict with social rules, or where the conflicts are blunted. For example, a man who is not in a position to hit his superior can compensate for this by hitting his wife. There are several variants of sadism and masochism, officially labelled as sexual perversions, which are in reality simply an outlet for the particularist desire for possession, realised within the permitted limits (this does not only apply to sex, of course — one needs simply to consider the sadism of war, in which anything is permitted against the enemy).

Where morality and relationships between the sexes are concerned, however, there is a special problem which must be dealt with separately. When we noted how the incest taboo developed even before the birth of civilisation, we said that this is an expression of the pushing back of natural limits. But in relationships between the sexes, the pushing back of natural limits emerges, from the theoretical point of view, in a form which is different from all other forms of human contact, precisely because it is the only human relation that is based on a biological (natural) drive. Of course nourishment is also a biological drive, but human contact is not of great importance to it. On the other hand, the natural drive which is at work in the relationship between mother

32

and baby is by definition (by nature) one between unequals. In the relationship between a mother and her grown-up children the natural limits become less and less effective. If grown-up children today stick to their mothers, it is usually on social and moral grounds: in other words, they form the relationships with their mother independently of the bond of biological kinship. The mother behaves in the same way with her grown-up children. The sex drive, on the other hand, is an absolute and unavoidable basis for contact between the sexes. It cannot be eliminated; it can only be humanised.

This is the origin of the special function of moral alienation in the regulation of relationships between the sexes. In fact moral norms either humanise or repress the sex drive — there is no third alternative. Freud's great merit was that he brought into the open the antagonism between moral norms and the sex drive, and all the deformations which are caused by repression of the sex drive. But since Freud considered the alienated social conditions to be the permanent fate of humanity, he did not think of the second alternative, the possibility of humanisation. Nevertheless, several aspects of this alternative could already be perceived in the prehistory of humanity.

Christianity, which for more than a thousand years was the main ideology determining morality, played a special role in humanising contact between the sexes and at the same time simply in suppressing the sex drive. The dual function of alienated morality can be observed here at its clearest. Let us consider humanisation first. Christianity accepted and proclaimed, though only as a tendency and as an ideology, the equality of man and woman before God. Women in the congregation are believers equal to men, and although they are excluded from the priesthood they can be canonised. Moral norms are also equal: virginity is a virtue for both man and woman, and adultery a sin. (The fact that this morality scarcely held good in practice is another question.) Without this equality at the ideological level, modern love — love springing from passion — would not have existed. However, the christian ethic is especially paradoxical when confronted with sexual relationships. In antiquity, the degree of humanisation in contacts between the sexes reflected the degree of moral development, while in the christian world the converse relation emerged: the greater the power of morality, the more was sexuality suppressed and even regarded at the ideological level as something "bestial". Even if the sexual act itself was permissible for the reproduction of the species, erotic enjoyment and sexual pleasure, and especially the cult of enjoyment, were sins, accompanied by guilt feelings. In this respect, bourgeois morality took the place of christian morality at least in part, and especially in relation to women; but on the other hand, in contrast to christianity, the inequality of women became a principle. The brothel became a bourgeois institution, linked with monogamy.

It is thus no accident that what is known as "the sexual revolution" is one of the main forms of expression of the revolt against bourgeois morality. The "sexual revolution" has already gone through several waves, but none of them has been so sweeping as that which has broken out in the West European student movements. Of course, it is not a unified movement but one in which several tendencies come together. However, we can distinguish two main tendencies. The first of these elevates into an ideological principle everything that has ever been practised in periods of dissolving moral norms: it identifies humanity with the "particularist" individual and demands absolute satisfaction. This is how sexual perversions, and chiefly sado-masochism (whose particularist character we have already referred to), become ideals. In my opinion, it is the other tendency which is important. Its partisans regard the sexual revolution as a means for ending alienation, which is their goal. They are not content with proclaiming the right of all human beings to pleasure (which is one of Marcuse's theses in *Eros and Civilisation*), but believe openly in equality between men and women in relationships between the sexes. Furthermore, they seek to eliminate from this relationship one of the chief forms of expression of alienation, namely the desire for possession. Those who seek to achieve this goal by means of the sexual revolution are proclaiming the possibility of a humanised society, even though there is much that is absurd and even naive in their theory and practice.

34

We have already pointed out that forms of humanised relationships between the sexes appear even under conditions of alienation, though only as an exception of course. The essential things in this respect are individual love and the norm, which has prevailed for some time, that marriage should be based on love. Connected with this there is the cultivation of the erotic, the comradeship and friendship of the couple (these two things are not the same), and the attempts of individual people to learn how to overcome the drive for possession and to fight against jealousy. Life and literature both offer us several examples: there is Chernyshevsky's Diary, for example, where the writer shows how his fight against jealousy played an important part in his revolutionary attitude as a whole.

Obviously, all the positive elements which tend towards the development of species-being can assume inhuman forms and in other respects play a destructive role. This is true of comradeship and friendship: the comradeship with which Lady Macbeth identifies with her husband is clearly not a good moral example. Not infrequently, this kind of degradation is accompanied by a love relationship too. Passionate love often sweeps aside all hindrances (including live human beings). But it is not the passion itself which is guilty, but preconceived ideas and a system of prejudices rooted in the human psyche which put hindrances in the path of passion (reasons of state, for example, as in Racine's *Bérénice*, or the possessiveness of passion in his *Phèdre*). Love is not independent in other respects of the whole social and human framework in which it arises: people generally fall in love with those who can serve their interests. In a class society, it is exceptional for love to cross social boundaries. George Bernard Shaw's play *Widowers' Houses* demonstrates this. Love relationships are inseparable from financial relationships, both in marriage, where the woman is usually maintained by the man, and in prostitution. In the twentieth century, love has become a social custom, an almost "obligatory" element of "good manners". The mass media and the cinema manipulate love for lucrative ends, just as they manipulate sexuality.

35

Clearly the depth or superficiality of love is only an expression of the greater or lesser depth of the human essence. The relative prevalence of the passionate kind of love coincides historically with the development of human subjectivity in its positive sense, with the birth of modern bourgeois individualism (modern love poetry is the most beautiful expression of this change). The more value an individual has (in the domain of feelings, ethics and culture), the richer is the love of which he is capable. The more deprived, the more alienated an individual is, the less value has his love, and the more superficial and impersonal it is.

However, one cannot regard the twentieth-century cult of love and sexuality as a merely artificial product of deliberate manipulation. In fact, in a world of loosening and breaking community links, where people are isolated and defenceless, love (together with sexuality) is the only direct and human relationship in which one individual person can meet another. Even the poorest love has some of the joy of finding another person, and at least temporarily weakens or banishes the feeling of loneliness and isolation, by building a bridge between two souls. Thus even the most commercialised relationships between the sexes express a part of the human essence and to a certain extent contribute to its preservation.

Let us briefly discuss now what is called "sexual morality". If we raise once again the question of whether the existence of some kind of "sexual morality" is a lasting value, our answer is a categorical "no". This is not simply because the existence of all partial or restricted moralities (this holds true not only of sexual morality but also of "business ethics" or "political morality") is an expression of moral alienation. A considerable section of public opinion still maintains that whatever goes against the prevailing sexual customs is "immoral". Furthermore, the concept of immorality often serves to describe the violation of customs concerning sexuality. On the other hand, if we examine the question from the point of view of the development of species-being (and here the problem of future tendencies appears), it becomes clear that in relationships between the sexes the only factors which harm universal values are those which harm all other spheres of morality. Breaking the will of another person by force, consciously misleading them, utilising them as a mere means to a goal, destroying another's life, the refusal of give-and-take and equality: these are attitudes and actions which, in contacts between the sexes, harm the universal human values irreparably and to the highest degree. But obviously these attitudes and actions are not specific transgressions of the special rules of some sexual morality, since they also transgress against species-being in all the spheres of human relations.

Our first assertion concerning the future, therefore, is that the system of specific norms of sexual morality will disappear, and that contact between the sexes in the future will be judged by the very same moral criteria as all the other spheres of human relationships.

We have assumed a kind of future society in which there is no alienation, and we foresee the end of alienation in relationships between the sexes as in all the other spheres that have been analysed so far. What picture do we have of these relationships, and what are their preconditions?

First of all, social inequality between man and woman will cease. This does not mean, of course, that all the forms of inequality will disappear, because the inequality between human beings cannot be eliminated in other spheres either. By the end of social inequality, we do not only mean that the social situation and starting conditions in life will be equal, but also that the distinction between characteristics which appear "natural" because we have grown used to them over thousands of years will gradually weaken and disappear: for example, the inequality between men and women with regard to sexual pleasure and the choice of partner, their intellectual activity, and emotional and moral attributes such as the "natural toughness" and rationality of man in contrast to the "natural" softness and emotional nature of woman, etc.

If life in general no longer revolves around property, possessiveness will disappear from relationships between the sexes. The "other" will no longer be an object of prestige, a trophy or a means to some end. In the relationships of really free individuals, the other is always an end in his or herself.

A love relationship can only come to an end if one of the two partners no longer feels the need, just as only mutual need can bring it about. Clearly this cannot eliminate suffering. Unrequited or unequally felt desires or loves will always be a source of pain and sometimes of tragedy. But what will disappear is the trauma which springs from the frustration of the desire for possession. The forsaken individual will suffer, but the pain will be entirely personal: it will not be wounded vanity, injured "honour", or a feeling that "one's property has been stolen". There will no longer be the catastrophes caused by breaches of sexual morality, just as there will be no sin, and no guilt feelings arising from the supposed transgression of some sexual code. Disappointment in love will thus become a suffering which is worthy of human beings.

In a non-alienated world, where the tendency to possessiveness no longer dominates, people will cease to be structured in a particularist way. The Individual personality, who has so far been an exception, will become typical of society. Moral norms will no longer confront a personality which is confirmed in its particularism as if they are something "alien". The personality will be capable of making value-oriented decisions as a result of its own endowments (natural abilities, talents and feelings) and to humanise its inclinations rather than suppress them.

We have seen that this is specially significant in sexuality, where the natural drives cannot be eliminated, but must be either suppressed or humanised. The individual no longer finds it necessary to suppress his physical needs, because these needs are humanised. We have already referred to the criteria of this humanisation: equality, mutuality, freedom of choice, and the refusal to treat others as means. Thus even a purely sexual attraction can be quite human, if it satisfies these criteria, just as today even the most "spiritual" love can be inhuman if it does not satisfy them. The borderline between the human and the inhuman is thus not where traditional (chiefly christian) morality draws it: it does not run between the "merely physical" and the "spiritual".

If we say that all human beings will be Individuals, capable of humanising their feelings, we certainly do not mean that everyone will love or desire equally and with the same intensity. Quite the contrary: everyone humanises their drives according to the criteria mentioned above, and these drives can be very varied. But fully developed Individuals will not need the norms of "sexual morality" in order to guide their drives in a human direction. Everyone knows best what relationship or relationships are most suitable for them. We have seen that before the beginning of civilisation, relationships between the sexes were characterised by an extraordinary many-sidedness. This many-sidedness developed within the clans and tribes, and thus had nothing universal about it. In the society of the future this many-sidedness will arise again, but this time on an individual basis, and thus it will be universal throughout: the Individual will, in his existence, be immediately embodying the universality of the human species in this respect.

So far we have only discussed the wealth of types of relationship between the sexes. We must also say something about the content of these relationships. We have said that the depth and the value of relationships between the sexes depend directly on the depth and general value of human beings. The richer the emotional, moral and intellectual culture, and the more all-embracing the intensity of the feelings, then the richer and deeper will be the emotional and intellectual relationships in contacts between the sexes too.

The perspectives which we have outlined undoubtedly imply the disappearance of monogamous marriage, characterised by alienation and based on property. Its monogamous form is that which for centuries has officially sanctioned the cohabitation of a man and a woman for life. The dissolution of monogamous marriage is a phenomenon which we can already see happening: it is a fact of our times. But the simple dissolution of monogamy in no way means that new and better relationships will necessarily arise. For this to happen a social movement is necessary, one whose goal is to get rid of all forms of alienation. As long as man and woman are not really equal, the dissolution of marriage will involve greater disadvantages for the woman, at least for a time. As long as we are still waiting for a new, really integrated human sense of com-

39

munity to be created, the dissolution of monogamy simply brings loneliness into focus and thus makes it more painful, even if it does not increase it. In spite of the painful conflicts which the dissolution of monogamous, alienated marriage brings, we consider this to be a process which in the long term points to a better future. It diminishes the role of proprietary and financial relations in the cohabition of the sexes and in extra-marital relationships, and it thereby reduces prostitution (this is especially true of the socialist societies). Of course, as long as a "naturally given" division of labour (to use Marx's words) exists, considerations of property and money cannot be removed from the relation between the sexes. But the motivational power of these factors can diminish, and in fact is doing so. The nineteenth-century marxists such as Engels and Bebel foresaw and approved of this aspect of the dissolution of alienated monogamy. What Engels and Bebel did not foresee were the conflicts and contradictions which accompany this dissolution, for they considered socialism to be a type of society which is composed of integrated groups from the beginning.

We have repeatedly emphasised that people of the future will choose the types and the content of their relationships on an individual basis, without their drives being fettered and suppressed by the inhibitions of sexual morality. But this clearly does not mean that the person who acts can ever himself be the sole judge of his actions. Even the most developed Individual can take mistaken decisions which stand in opposition to the requirements of universal values, or can sometimes act contrary to what is deeply human in him; and besides this, there will never be a point at which all Individuals are equally developed. Thus there will always be a judge and a judgement, i.e. the public opinion of communities which are based on relationships between free and equal human beings. This public opinion, however, will be different from all previous kinds of public judgement, in that it will not be based on particularist norms which are hostile to individuals and based on mere custom. It will judge according to the case and the situation. Its sole criterion will be to find out whether the decision under consideration harms the general values which obtain at the given level of development of species-being, and whether it might have been possible — and at what price — for the individual not to have harmed them. Thus the judgement of public opinion will not have the effect of suppressing individual drives, but of humanising them.

Fourier and, following him, Marx said that the relationships between man and woman are a yardstick of the humanisation of a society. We have outlined here the perspective of a humanised society which for the first time in history permits humanised relationships between men and women. But we do not deny (in fact we pointed to it at the beginning) that a different perspective is equally possible. In a world which is open to all kinds of manipulation, everything that points today to the creation of values can produce an opposite and undesirable outcome. If, for example, the dissolution of monogamy or the sexual revolution point to a more human future, they can equally point to the beginning of the defeat of values which humanity has built up gradually. The individual who is manipulated by his particularist motivations can sink deeper into falsity in his relationships with the opposite sex than the ascetic who suppresses his drives or the libertine who pursues his passions blindly and without thought for others. The pseudo-scientific and literary prattle about the sex-life, the "technical" and at the same time conformist advice, based on the principle that "everybody does it", degrades sexuality to a deeper extent than the anguish of feeling guilty about the shame of sexual activity. (To avoid being misunderstood, we should make it clear that these remarks are not directed against sex education!) In fact this kind of manipulation falsifies Individuality, which is the most valuable quality in the relationship between the sexes whether it refers to sexuality, or to the erotic, or to love.

If we make a choice in respect of social conflicts, we are at the same time opting for a certain kind of future for relationships between the sexes. We choose free and equal (and of course individual) relationships, relationships which in all spheres of human life are innocent of any tendency to possessiveness, and are notable for their wealth, their depth and their sincerity.

41

3
Agnes Heller

MARX'S THEORY OF REVOLUTION AND THE REVOLUTION IN EVERYDAY LIFE

In the last twenty years, the concept of everyday life has emerged among several marxist thinkers who are relatively independent of each other. We need only refer, in historical order of the emergence of the problem, to Lefebvre, Lukács and Kosik. It has been a reaction to the new problems which sprang up in the course of revolutionary practice (as is also true of every single other enrichment of marxism's conceptual apparatus), even if some of these problems were not evident. This new aspect of revolutionary practice has emerged in both the capitalist and the socialist world. In the capitalist world, it coincides with the abrupt end of the period of optimism and illusions that followed the defeat of fascism, the period when the overthrow of fascism had failed to bring about a new, left-oriented Europe. What is more, this was the end of the period which Thomas Mann called "the age of the morally good", in which the collective fight against oppression and complete dehumanisation afforded people a sense of community, an immediate goal to fight for and a moral stance, and which brought about so many important examples of heroism and solidarity. The new bourgeois "establishment" restored the world of bourgeois everyday life, and in fact strengthened it. The new stage of industrial development made it appear as if the social forces which had till then been thought of as revolutionary, and particularly the working class, had been integrated into capitalist development, and had taken up the alienated way of living which this society offered it, along with the rise in their living standards and the increased

42

satisfaction of their needs. The relative and temporary success of the manipulation of needs and the manipulation of public opinion has lent a central importance to the critique of everyday life and thinking. In the socialist world, the same problem became acute in the period following Stalin's death. Here, it became clear that although the mere removal of stalinist power was the indispensable condition for the formation of a humanised way of life, it was far from being a sufficient one. For in those countries where this removal was carried out (more or less successfully), the issue of the formative function of the socialist way of life was, like other issues, still unresolved.

It is an undoubted and often emphasised fact that Marx not only saw the revolution as the seizure of power by the revolutionary proletariat, but regarded all this (the negative abolition of private property) as the precondition for the process which he termed the positive abolition of private property, and thus of alienation. This also signifies the radical re-structuring of everyday life. It is likewise an undoubted and often emphasised fact that the individual human being in everyday life considers his environment to be "already given"; that he appropriates the system of habits and manipulation of this environment spontaneously; that his behaviour is pragmatic (thus the essential thing for him is that which guarantees the success of a given activity); that his concepts are the lowest common denominator; that his knowledge, measured by the standards of philosophy, is mere opinion. Moreover, it is a fact that everyday life is composed of heterogeneous types of activity, and that these types of activity are never directly related to human practice as a whole. Our question is as follows. If we accept all these structural facts as true, and take them as our basis, is everyday life necessarily alienated — and, therefore, is a radical re-structuring of everyday life possible, alongside the continuation of its structural basis?

In order that individuals may reproduce society, it is necessary for them to reproduce themselves as individuals. Everyday life is the totality of those activities which characterise the constant capacity for social reproduction through individual reproductions. No society can exist without individual reproduction, and no individuals can exist without their own self-reproduction. Thus there is an everyday life in *every* society — otherwise there is no society. Equally, every person has an everyday life, whatever their position in the social division of labour.

In the historical epochs which preceded civilisation, what existed was (though with certain limitations) *only* everyday life, inasmuch as the process of maintaining the species and that of maintaining the individual were still scarcely, if at all, separate. The major objectivations of society as a whole — labour (as the necessary basic activity for the reproduction of society), science, politics, law, religion, philosophy and art — broke free during the development of private property and the alienation of everyday life. The separation between everyday life and the objectivations conforming to the species thus reflects two processes which historically were contemporaneous but which are not connected in principle. One is the relative autonomisation of the immediate relation to conformity with the species; historically speaking this is definitive and irrevocable. The other is the split between the development of the species-being and the individual person (the individual person from a whole group or class of people) and thus the achievement of the first process *in the form of alienation*. It undoubtedly seems like retrograde utopianism to assert a historical perspective in which everyday life once again integrates the objectivations immediately conforming to the species. On the other hand, recognition of the alternative to such a future, from the point of view of the status quo in which the alienation between everyday life and objectivations immediately conforming to the species is regarded as definitive, would point to the tasks of revolutionary theory. This is, moreover, the case with every technocratic world-view, though the concept is not clearly stated: it believes that the problems of human destiny can be solved simply by means of the development of productive capacity, science, and the increased satisfaction of people's everyday needs. At the same time, one would likewise consider utopian any revolutionary demand which sought to remove this discrepancy by raising the totality of everyday life to the sphere of activities (i.e. objectivations) immediately conforming to the species. There will never exist a type of humanity (and this can never be the case, in principle) in which individuals

44

do not have to reproduce themselves, and in which this self-reproduction does not stake a claim to a relatively large part of the individual's activity. There cannot and never will be a type of humanity in which individuals can give a philosophical basis to all those activities which are connected with their own existence and with their movement in the given system of need. People will simply not be physically capable (and they never are) of living the kind of life in which they call in question *everything* that is already given and established, or in which — in some part of their everyday life — they make decisions which are not based on generalised categories, analogies or impulses. I believe that the essence of the alienation of everyday life is not fundamentally rooted in everyday forms of thought and action, but in the way in which *the relation of the individual to these forms of activity* emerges, and in the question of whether he is capable or not of hierarchising these forms of activity in an independent way and of synthesising them into a unity. In fact this capability depends on what kind of relation the individual has to the non-everyday, i.e. to the various objectivations conforming to the species.

In its prehistory humanity worked out, at least as a tendency, all those values which can serve as the foundation for its "true history". If we examine the history of humanity we can form the conclusion that the behaviour of the subject of everyday life, i.e. the individuals who live everyday life, can be distinguished by two main types: Particularity and Individuality. To clarify the point: these are two extreme types, and the transitional stages between them are many.

Marx writes, in the *Economic and Philosophic Manuscripts of 1844*:

"Conscious life-activity distinguishes man immediately from animal life-activity. Only because of this is he a species-being. Only because of this is he a conscious being, i.e. his own life is an object to him, because he is a species-being. Only because of this is his activity free activity. Alienated labour reverses the relation, so that because man is a conscious being, he turns his life-activity, his being, into a means for his existence."

45

Thus man's conscious nature, i.e. the attribute which conforms to his species, becomes at the same time the means for the revocation of his species-being, for it turns his being [*Wesen*] into the instrument of his existence. It is precisely this that forms the particular, alienated person. The goal of the particular person is the maintenance of his own self: he identifies himself spontaneously with the whole system of customs and requirements which make his mere self-maintenance possible, conflict-free and "comfortable". However, it is not inevitable that *everyone* without exception and to the same extent carries out this exchange of means and end. There are (or can) always be those who fight to regard themselves, their individual being, as conforming to the species, and to behave as species-beings; thus from the point of view of that which conforms with the species, i.e. of the stage of development conforming with the species which has been reached at a given point in time, they consider themselves as *object*, and do not unconditionally identify themselves with the needs of their own existence or make their own essential capacities the means for the satisfaction of their existential needs. The Individual is the person whose own life consciously becomes an object for him, since he is consciously a species-being.

Precisely because the Individual has a conscious relation to conformity with the species, he is capable of "ordering" his everyday life *too*, on the basis of this conscious relation (of course, this happens under given conditions and possibilities). The Individual is a person who "synthesises" in himself the chance uniqueness of his individuality with the universal generality of the species.

The expression "synthesise" is very important. Of course, every person is at the same time both unique and generally in conformity with the species. But the merely particular person behaves towards both his uniqueness and the forms of objectivation of general conformity with the species (i.e. towards the immediate environment, the community and its requirements) as towards a "transcendent given". The becoming of the Individual begins where this quasi-transcendence ceases — but in *both* relationships. I may be merely discontented with my "fate", or I may be discontented simply with myself alone —

46

but this does not necessarily lead towards my becoming an Individual. The overcoming of this quasi-transcendence signifies a *regular interaction* between the Individual and his world. Every person forms his world and thus himself too. The re-structuring of the world and of himself (and the carrying out of a synthesis of both) is not, however, the motivation of every person. When it becomes my motivation to re-structure myself and my world, to objectivate my capabilities, and to "absorb" into myself the capabilities and modes of behaviour conform-ing with the species which have formed in the areas open to me, only then am I on the way to becoming an Individual.

Every person has an *I-consciousness*, just as he also has knowledge of what conforms with the species. But only the Individual has *self-consciousness*. Self-consciousness is the I-consciousness mediated by the consciousness of what conforms with the species. Whoever has self-consciousness does not identify spontaneously with his own self: he stands at a dis-tance from himself and therefore from his particular motives, attitudes and given elements. He "cultivates" not only and not primarily those given elements which help him to obtain a better orientation and esteem in his immediate environment (as the particular person does), but also those which he con-siders more valuable, which correspond to the hierarchy of values *chosen* from the objectivations conforming to the species, from the social system of needs.

In the prehistory of humanity, in order for a person to be able to live his everyday life, it was *sufficient* for his way of life to be oriented to particularity. However, for anyone to be-come an Individual, he had constantly to exceed the merely everyday: his conscious relation to the I and to integration with the species could not come about within the framework of the everyday *alone*. This does not mean, though, that Individuality did not always play a role, nor sometimes a quite exemplary one, in the organising of everyday life. The Individual organises his everyday life in such a way as to impress upon it the mark of that Individuality which has sprung from the synthesis between his individually given elements and that which con-forms with the species. Within the possibilities given by the social division of labour, the framework of the way of life and

47

the value system which operates, Individuality develops that consciously formed relation to the conditions of life which, following Goethe, we shall call "life-conduct".

It is possible to put the everyday life of the Individual under the heading of "life-conduct". But although "life-conduct" is the category which everyday life falls into, the only person capable of "life-conduct", i.e. of synthesising himself into an Individual, is he who stands in a conscious relation to the objectivations which conform with the species (and to *any* of these objectivations): that is, a conscious species-being.

However, all this does not mean that the basic categories of everyday life cease to exist for the Individual. The same basic categories and structures exist: but in the synthesis of life-conduct, they have another meaning. The Individual is born into a given system of manipulations and customs, just as the particular person is. And the person who is in the process of becoming an Individual, too, accepts as given the conventions which function as a system of social relations and the system of manipulation, and he too adapts himself to them. He learns to speak his mother tongue without having the faintest idea about linguistics. He adapts himself to customs and the handling of his affairs. The particular person and the Individual drive cars, use lifts (the existence of which they regard as natural), spend their money in department stores, all in complete ignorance of theories of finance. There is "merely" one distinction between them (and the word "merely" signifies in fact a whole world of difference), and this is that for the Individual the totality of "given" world does not have a quasi-transcendent appearance; rather, this appearance continually dissolves, in the proportion to which he becomes an Individual. Thus the Individual is capable or rather becomes capable of discerning, in the already given structures of everyday life, those factors and demands which hinder his development in conformity with the species, which have become pure formalities, or which conceal aspirations and interests with a negative value-content: it is *these* things which he rids himself of, rejects or by-passes. Let us repeat: this should never be regarded as identical with the by-passing or negation of the structure of everyday life. The ideological factor, which the Individual uses

48

in order to make a choice from within the structure of customs of everyday activities, is simply his *Weltanschauung*.

The *Weltanschauung* is not simply ideology, it is an individual ideology; it is the image of the world (constructed in the last analysis out of philosophical and ethical concepts) with which a person orders his own individual activity in the totality of practice. To this extent, and only to this extent, the everyday life of the Individual assumes a philosophical character, his life-conduct is "guided" by his *Weltanschauung*.

So far we have been speaking about the everyday life of persons (whether particular or individual persons), and we have thus been abstracting from those concrete integrations in the framework of which everyday life flows. Since the problem of the Individual and integration is very complex, historically variable, and raises very many problems which go beyond the framework of this essay, we should simply limit ourselves to the question which is closely related to our perspective, that of the revolutionary re-structuring of everyday life.*

The particular person "lives in" his world, spontaneously, while the Individual on the other hand has a life-conduct which is ordered by his *Weltanschauung*. The *Weltanschauung* is not, however, simply a view of the world, but (as we have already said) an individual ideology, which aims to settle conflicts and is oriented towards the conscious re-structuring or conservation of reality. This re-structuring can of course cover a wide spectrum; it can have an ethical character, or that of revolutionary practice. It follows from all this that there is only one case in which Individual life-conduct can also be "individualistic": that is, where the *Weltanschauung* which ordains his life-conduct is utility raised to the level of a principle, and where "possession", transformed into a *Weltanschauung*, is the very principle of this utility. This attitude is typical of members of the ascendant bourgeoisie. Where, on the other hand, the principle of "possession" does not ordain life-conduct, *the Individual without community cannot exist*: the community is always there, whether in reality or in thought.

---

*For a fuller analysis of this question, see Agnes Heller, "Individual and Community" in *Social Praxis*, vol. 1 no. 1.

The particular person can live in the world of pure mediation, since he constantly chooses, from the mediated relations conceived as quasi-transcendental and from the integrations into which he was born (nation, class, layer, etc.), whatever corresponds to his momentary interests, his self-preservation and his comfort; he is a being that acts in common, but he is not a communal being. The Individual, however, defetishises the world; his *Weltanschauung* is choice, and this choice signifies precisely that he decides on a community. The shaping of the life-conduct and the choice of community are two sides of the same process. The community is not simply a political association, although it is often that too. It is the simultaneous and sudden creation of immediate human relations in a world of mediation. The creation of these immediate human relations (we can only speak of immediacy in a relative sense) makes it possible to carry out a task which has an indivisible quality: the re-structuring of reality in such a way that in so doing we can order our lives in their totality along lines worthy of human beings. (Only since the emergence of the Individual of the modern era can we speak of the freely chosen community as a universal phenomenon. The ancient and medieval Individual, at least in the vast majority of cases, was born into a community.)

I should like now to turn back to our initial problem. In so far as we, as revolutionary marxists, maintain our goal of bringing about a non-alienated society, we should be proposing not the abolition of everyday life but the creation of a non-alienated everyday life. And it is not only a question of proposing it, but (within the given possibilities) of realising it. This does not mean repeating the illusion which Schiller first outlined on the topic of aesthetic education, which regards the shaping of a good life-conduct among individuals as a programme that has to be carried out *before* the economic and political re-structuring. And we regard as a similarly metaphysical illusion the idea that we must first abolish economic and political alienation in order to be able to humanise everyday human relations *post festum*. This was the illusion of the French Enlightenment, to which the idea of the enlightened sovereign necessarily belongs, the utopia of the great law-giver

50

who undertakes these preliminaries and "introduces" the transformation. Marx showed us different perspectives in the *Theses on Feuerbach*. We ourselves are in a position to re-structure our society economically and politically in a direction that leads to the positive abolition of alienation; but we can only carry out this task if we are capable, within the given possibilities, of abolishing the *subjective aspects* of alienation: if we fight not only for the transformation of institutions but also for the re-structuring of our own everyday life, and if we shape the kind of communities which will lend a meaning to our lives and at the same time set an example.

Marx regarded communism as movement. As movement, communism is a *permanent* struggle for the abolition of exploitation and private property. Its character as movement includes not only the concept of permanence, not only the constant surpassing of specific goals, but also the activity of every person taking part in this movement. As movement, communism allows every person taking part in it to become conscious of the goals which conform to the species; individual persons of communism, as members of a movement, can only be Individuals, or they must at least be in the process of becoming Individuals. And conversely, today it is only within the framework of a communist movement that one can find and develop an Individual life-conduct that also has a mass character. At the moment, a section among the communist parties has lost sight of the goal which Marx set: instead of being a movement, they have taken the form of traditional parties, and this in spite of the fact that the need for a real marxist movement is growing. I repeat that nothing but a communist movement in Marx's sense can guide the prevailing discontent with the traditional forms of everyday life in the direction of the creation of a humanised society.

If we take a look at the student movements which have broken out in all parts of the world in recent years, we can see that their political ideologies can be quite different, but what is identical about them is the fact that they are oriented towards changing the world. They are not related to one political ideology. Behind the movements there lies a discontent with everyday life and at the same time a demand, which is

51

inseparable from this discontent, for an Individual life-conduct and for immediate human relations. One might refer here to the communes of Berlin or to Cohn-Bendit's interview with Sartre. If marxist revolutionaries are to understand these movements, and especially if they are to be directed towards the positive abolition of alienation, it is not enough to launch political slogans, however progressive these may be. The question is (and of course it is only one among many), can we offer a new way of life? And what kind of a way of life can we offer? This is as important in capitalism, where the goal is to defeat the social system, as it is in socialism, in which the effort is towards reform.

It does not lie within the scope of this essay to formulate a programme in this direction. In any case, I could not do so. I should simply like to point out some of the problems which arise in this context.

One question is that of the ideal. It is an undoubted fact that among the youth movements seeking new ways of life today, Che Guevara stands at the peak of the hierarchy of ideals. The fact that he stands at this peak is not only understandable, it is a satisfactory state of affairs. I find only one problem with it, and this is that his function as an ideal has assumed an exclusive character, and therefore there is a lack of pluralism in ideals. There is no need to waste many words describing what is understandable and satisfactory about the persistent influence of Guevara. Not only did he leave "home" (to put it figuratively) in order to dedicate himself to the revolution, but later he also renewed his choice: he renounced power so that he could die as a simple Bolivian guerrilla. The fact that he has become an ideal points also to a commitment to a revolutionary perspective. However, a movement needs not only symbolic ideals but real ones too. Even the revolutionary is not and cannot be embodied in an attitude of one kind only. We need only look at Lenin, whose symbolic revolutionary essence was only expressed through many years of prosaic activity and who, in contrast to Guevara, took over a position of power on behalf of the revolution. Guevara is a symbolic ideal, for a young person (or even an older one) who decides to dedicate himself to the revolution cannot repeat Guevara's fate except in very unusual cases. To follow him on a mass scale is almost as impossible as for a christian to follow Christ. The autocracy of the mythical ideal is linked with the real danger that those who accept this ideal on its own may tend to conduct their lives in the false appearance of an unobtainable image, as their forefathers did. The Kierkegaardian paradox, that one may follow the path of Christ but that no one will perceive it because to "outside" appearances one lives like a philistine, is only too true. And this is not some mere ideological question, it is an extraordinarily real problem. The German or French youth who works as a technician in a factory or as a doctor in a hospital is, in principle, incapable of living Guevara's kind of life. And if he has no plurality of ideals and no system of values, he will live like other people. If, however, it is possible to introduce an ideology into the movements "from outside", then I believe that this also holds true for ideals. I should like to refer to someone who in my opinion represents a real ideal, C. Wright Mills. The form of behaviour which he formulated and elaborated was that when one lives in an undemocratic environment, one should think and act as if one were in a real democracy. The fundamental bravery of this way of life is not military heroism but *civic courage*. Whoever says no to the dominant prejudices and to the oppressing power, and when necessary (and it is often necessary) to public opinion, and practices this throughout his life and in his life-conduct, is someone who has the virtue of civic courage. Of course, C. Wright Mills and civic courage are only one example, and only one real ideal. I repeat: there is a need for a plurality of ideals, and without this the movement of discontent with everyday life can lead to fiasco.

The other question which must be briefly touched on is the cult of sexuality. I shall not refer at the moment to its manipulated forms, since that is not our topic: I shall refer rather to the sex-cult which springs from the real need to re-structure the way of life. This is a phenomenon which has already been in existence for decades, and its common features are likewise decades old: the revolt against monogamy, against the way of thinking which links it with property and possession and against the prevailing system of prejudices, all of which are so well-known that we need not waste too many words on them here. Since the second world war, a new aspect and motive has been added to those mentioned above. As a result of the concrete forms assumed by modern industrial development, immediate human relations have been "squeezed out" of all the spheres of life in European and North American society. Natural communities, i.e. those which are not chosen, have lost their intimacy (it is only in childhood that the family still casts an aura of intimate community), and the change in the nature of labour makes it increasingly impossible for such communities to be formed immediately in the labour process. The need for immediacy of human relations has not been lost, however, and this demand can be satisfied only in love. But the impoverishment of immediate human relation leaves its mark also on the concrete content of the love life: in the last analysis it is sex alone, above all, that enables an immediate union to be established. Nothing is more ridiculous than to confront this process with the moral admonitions of our parents. One should not simply preach about "sex not being the only thing in the world"; one should (and here I return to my point of departure) bring about the kind of human communities in which completely new ways of life, containing numerous types of immediacy and a sexuality freed from the instinct for possession, can develop.

It is beyond question that the humanised ways of life cannot be reduced to a rational way of spending "free time", nor to a rational organisation of consumption and enjoyment within this free time. At the same time, I believe it to be utopian to consider that one must bring about humanistic living communities by first humanising the labour process. At today's level of industrial development, especially in those countries where the level of industrialisation is lower, the majority of jobs are carried out under degrading conditions, and this may hold true for a long time in the future — we do not know how long. The humanisation of the labour process, under given conditions, can of course be part of a programme; and furthermore, the striving for optimisation in socialist society must continue to set the humanisation of the labour process as a goal, but without the illusion that this can be the yardstick for the humanisation of life as a whole. This kind of illusion can easily turn the movement into the instrument of subtle manipulation. The central programme for the humanisation of life is situated in the sphere of labour but *outside the labour process*: in actual (not manipulated) "participation", in accountability and democracy at the workplace.

We have noted that marxist revolutionaries must recognise the extraordinary significance of the claim to new ways of life and of the need for community, and that they should help the movement of those who seek a new way of life and society, aimed at the positive abolition of private property. We have also noted that the humanisation of the labour process is not a real point of departure here. The real points of departure are, in my opinion, of an ethical and political nature. The ethical aspect of the problem is that one must help to formulate a programme which is directed against proprietary ways of life and the proprietary psychology. Marx described the "particular" person of class society by saying that his entire meaning is reduced to that of "possession", and that the new communities must revolt against "possession", against the proprietary psychology and the fetishisation of the "thing". One must formulate and clarify the distinction between possession and enjoyment, and thus announce a programme for the conduct of a "good life" without falling into aestheticism.

All these ethical factors, alone and in themselves, do not have a community-forming character, and even if this were the case, the resulting communities would last only for a very short time. The ethical critique of the old ways of life can only have a lasting, community-forming effect if it is based on a unified view of the world. And in a unified view of the world, political commitment constantly plays a central role. It is by no means an accident that the formulation of the demand for the new way of life is linked everywhere with the adoption of certain positions on political questions. One of these decisive questions in recent years has been the Vietnam war and solidarity with the Third World. Much more problematical and unclear is the relation between these very heterogeneous and disparate movements and the political character of their own countries. Usually they have no definite political programme (one cannot expect this from them), they do not always have a political goal, and yet they always stand in some *relation* to politics. Behind their slogans or vaguely formulated desires there is always the programme inscribed on the banners of the French revolution: Liberty, Fraternity, Equality. Many groups emphasise liberty, while others put more emphasis on equality. But a lasting, life-shaping community does not exist without a relatively concrete, definite political activity and everyday political work, which makes it possible to go beyond the mere regulation of free time (i.e. consumption) and achieve a life-conduct determined by the *Weltanschauung*. Marxist revolutionaries must act in an exemplary way here, by analysing the real ways and possibilities for the creation of freedom and equality in the various social systems, and thus creating a theoretical basis for the formation of such kinds of *Weltanschauung* as are oriented towards guiding the everyday life of the various communities by the norms of a non-alienated society.

I believe that in the capitalist societies it all depends on the overthrow of the system, while in socialist societies it all depends on the creation of socialist democracy. A few words on this last point. The socialist societies, as *socialist* ones, cannot function at all unless there are communities which set themselves the goal of re-structuring reality and themselves. The active revolutionary marxists in socialist society must think about the creation of institutions which not only guarantee the right of the individual to freedom (bourgeois democracies do this too) but which, far beyond this, create the possibility for the activity of society as a whole to be based on the activity of communities which are themselves based on immediately human relationships. I do not believe that direct democracy is outdated, even at the present level of industrial development. There is no doubt that the form of decision-making in society as a whole (I emphasis the word "form") can in no way be directly democratic as it was in the ancient city-state. However, I insist that it is possible to work out such forms in an institutional way, and that these will make direct democracy effective at the level of society as a whole. What is true is that the condition for direct democracy has always been, everywhere, the relative equality of resources. And therefor I believe that the slogan of formal freedom, without any attention paid to a programme for equality, is a slogan which endangers freedom too, i.e. the real freedom which leads in actual fact to the positive abolition of private property.

To return to our initial problem: the constant revolutionising of everyday life is the goal, but it is also the precondition for socialism to be able to fulfil its historical task. And the marxist movements can only be revolutionary and exemplary within capitalism if, along with their political programme, they offer a new morality too, a new way of life.

4
Agnes Heller

THEORY AND PRACTICE FROM THE POINT OF VIEW OF HUMAN NEEDS

Theory and practice always belong to the same productive and social unit (structure), as its constructive elements. This explains why theory and practice in different societies differ not only in their content but also in the way in which they interact, so that the function of theory differs too. There are quite a few social units (one can find many examples for this even among the so-called "primitive societies" of the twentieth century) where theory and practice are not differentiated, but fulfil the function of social reproduction in an integral way. Thus, from the point of view of the problem presented here, one must not reduce the early-medieval and bourgeois societies to a common denominator. In the former christianity was not simply a homogeneous ideology, but penetrated the daily practice of men, whose conforming or divergent aims were motivated by, among other things, the hegemonic ideology. The general problem of the relation between practice and theory did not even emerge until the advent of bourgeois society. If it has emerged, it has never done more than simply raise the question why persons or groups of people did not realise their principles. However, this is not significant for our problem; at best, it is a secondary element of it.

So the *general* problem of the relation between theory and practice is a *particular* problem of bourgeois society, a product of its structure and of the manifestation of that structure. Therefore, precisely when the problem is posed in its most *general* form, we ought to be quite clear in our minds that we are confronting a particular problem, which is itself a product of history, and, as one might expect, bound to a *definite* historical period, however long and important that period is.

58

I would like to make it clear from the beginning that in the course of my argument I shall not be dealing with the relation between the theory of natural science and practice, although the rise of natural science, from Galileo on, constitutes an integral aspect of the process to which I refer. In the following pages I shall limit my analysis to the relation between social theory and practice.

Posing the problem of this relation is in itself the consequence and the expression of the division of labour and of commodity production. The formation of the intelligentsia, as a particular social stratum whose task is to "produce" theory, is a result of the division of labour. The social forces which create theory will be separate from those which realise it. This is true even if the theoretician represents the interests of a certain class directly, for in bourgeois society even quite divergent theories conform to the schema of commodity production. Whether they directly express the interests of a certain class or not, theories still in every case end up on the market. That not all products reach the market is a fact so obvious that it does not call for any analysis. Such discussion is made superfluous by the very fact that in the latter case — if we take the structure of capitalist society as it is — the theoretical product does not even have the opportunity to be transformed into practice. So I shall discard this aspect from the point of view of the problem in hand.

The principal form in which theory arrives on the market is publication. This is the way in which theory becomes available and can attract the consumer. There are secondary forms such as propaganda activities, which are either mediated by personal contact or, as is becoming increasingly the case, by the mass media, or by both. In free market systems theory also comes on to the free market, and human beings take it or leave it, utilise it or not, according to their needs. Under conditions of a manipulated market, free competition in theories must also be limited. Most theoretical products put into circulation on the market are from the outset designed to manipulate public opinion in a predetermined direction. And what is more: in the bourgeois society oppositional and even revolutionary theory is in most cases bound to follow the same route, since it is channelled in that direction by the structure of society. Marx's well-known statement that the theory which penetrates the masses becomes a material force, also presupposes — at least at some imaginary starting-point — the existence of masses influenced by the ideology of the dominant class, and a revolutionary theory without masses.

In consequence of the modern division of labour, the theoretician (it does not matter whether he is an economist, a philosopher or a sociologist) is someone who offers his theory on the market. As we are working with an abstract model, let us put his various motives in parentheses, and suppose that all these "men of theory" appear on the market with their theoretical products because they regard their ideologies and the points of view expressed in their theories as true. Let us suppose that in selling their theories they are not led by the mere desire to gain money and high positions but rather by the hope that the circulation or acceptance of their ideas will influence society, either the whole or certain parts of it, in a direction that they regard as preferable. Obviously, this is not true in the great majority of cases, but for the analysis of the relation between theory and practice any motivation divergent from this can be put into parentheses. At this point, the problem is to determine the identity of the "purchasers" of this commodity, how they buy it and what motives drive them to acquire what they do.

It is universally known that even if the appropriation of certain ideas assumes mass proportions, this does not necessarily imply that the theory finds its way, through these mediations, into practice. The majority of those who adhere to a theory are ordinary consumers, who consume a theory as they would a toothpaste. This mode of consumption is the so-called "general culture", a condition *sine qua non* for belonging to a given social stratum, just as using a certain brand of toothpaste. Of course, the level of consumption itself can act as an index. It can indicate which theories are on their way to being transformed into practice in certain strata, because the market demand for these theories usually increases. All the same, the more manipulated the market becomes, the less are indices of this kind reliable.

Since I am here analysing theory from the point of view of practice I must neglect all those "purchasers" who are consumers only in the above sense. Consequently, I have to limit my enquiry to an analysis of those who purchase theoretical products from the point of view of practice, their motives and the way in which they acquire theory.

This investigation, however, presupposes a previous definition of practice and of the practical efficacy of theory as well. It is possible to operate with a fairly general definition of the concept of practice which includes every type of social activity and, in the last analysis, human activity in general. This is one of the meaningful concepts of practice, but it does not make sense when one analyses practice precisely in its interaction with theory. If in fact we set out from so wide a definition of practice, all theoretical activities ought to be considered as practical activities as well, thus losing the *differentia specifica*.

That is why we have to find a more restricted definition for the concept of practice, without rejecting the general-ontological concept of *praxis*. At this point, however, we find ourselves confronted with a new difficulty, i.e. the impossibility of formulating an integrated definition for the concept of practice in this narrower sense. For these kinds of practice in the narrower sense can be interpreted only in relation to their corresponding theories.

In the development of my analysis I shall not take into consideration those ideologies that directly express an apologia for capitalist society, and I shall not deal with the corresponding practice which keeps the existing society working. I do not regard these ideologies as theories, even if they aspire to be such. As direct manifestations of false consciousness, they can be described as pseudo-theories, just as the corresponding practice, whose only function is to "keep things working", is a pseudo-practice.

The various kinds of practice, and the various types of theory that correspond to them, differ from each other according to their aims and also according to whether they are or at least try to be realised in mass action or not, and if they are, what kind of mass action this is. In this respect, the problem of "means" — and in particular, whether to use violence or not — has, in my view, no decisive importance. I am in fact convinced that if we put this problem above the others, a grasp of the *real* difference between the various types of theory and practice becomes impossible. Posed at this level of abstraction, the question whether the use of violence is right or wrong, is or is not admissible, is or is not necessary, seems to me altogether sterile. The dilemma can only be resolved concretely, from the standpoint of the aims and the character of the social movement of a certain practice and of a concrete situation. A given type of theory and practice always has its adequate means in every concrete situation. The use or avoidance of violence can be decided only by investigating whether its employment — and not in general, but in its concrete form — is or is not adequate for the aims and the movement of a given practice. It is not adequate if its use destroys the aims and the movement themselves or pushes them in a direction which diverges from the original intentions.

I repeat: I consider the aims and the character of the various movements as the real basis for classification. From this point of view we can distinguish the following types of practice.

(1) So-called *partial reform*: a type of activity that sets itself the task of transforming individual sectors, institutions, or relations of society. In this case the original intention is actually partial reform, i.e. reform that does not transcend the presuppositions of the given society. Reformist theories and activities of this type can be directed towards quite different kinds of sphere, for example towards the economic system, the political system, the legislative system or the educational system. The partial reforms are in most cases worked out by experts (who are in the sector affected), although it is not exclusively experts who take part in the formulation of the theories of these reforms. Partial reforms are generally preceded by "critical campaigns" directed against those institutions which are regarded as obsolete. In cases of partial reforms the mass base of the practice can be very slender, restricted to the activity of experts, although in the majority of cases the situation is otherwise. The greater the resistance shown to a partial reform, the greater is the degree of mass participation, partly by exercising "pressure", partly by taking part directly in the realisation of the

reform (consider, for example, the institutions of divorce in Italy). All the same, in these cases mass actions are accidental, and they cease to exist after the reform has been realised. Movements that aim at partial reforms can easily become vehicles of manipulation (even when that was not the intention of their initiators or executors) simply by reason of the fact that, by channelling dissatisfaction against the existing social system towards the reform of concrete (individual, partial) institutions, they create the appearance of the transformability of the given social order.

(2) *General reform.* This second type of practice sets itself the object of transforming the whole of society by means of partial reforms. The theoreticians of the movements of general reform are characterised by a *critical* attitude towards the whole of the dominant social system. They are not experts and even if they are, they do not act as such. They are rather the leaders of movements, or they appeal to movements embracing the whole society. Movements for general reform are — at least in their ideal types — movements with a large, organised mass base, and they do not cease to exist after realisation of a partial reform but remain permanently "in action". Examples of this type of practice are the pre-1914 social democratic movements.

(3) *Political revolutionary movements.* The aim of these is the radical transformation of the whole of society, and the decisive moment in this is the conquest of political power. This can be considered by them as their ultimate aim, although for most political revolutionary ideologies it constitutes the point of departure. The mass base of political revolutionary movements can vary greatly in its size. If it is restricted from the beginning, the possibilities of victory are scant. However, the mass base of victorious political revolutionary movements is twofold. The force that guides the movement is in most cases a minority, ready for any action, prepared to run any risk: a revolutionary élite, but at the same time enjoying active mass support. However, from the moment of political victory onwards, "the tide begins to flow the other way": the activity of the masses decreases and later turns into passivity. This is the course of all the political revolutions that have matured on

the terrain of bourgeois society (and political revolutions mature only on the terrain of this society). The purest, most classical example of this kind of political revolution is French Jacobinism.

To interpret this dynamic I must refer to Marx's famous formulation about the split in man between "bourgeois" and "citizen". The "natural" existence of human beings in capitalist society is that of the bourgeois, of the private person who struggles for his own direct interests. This is evidently an alienated existence, since it is (among other things) the abandonment of any attempt to transform society. Citizen-existence is no less alienated, in so far as activity in this political sphere is separated from everyday life: above all from the everyday life of other people, but from the citizen's own life too. In the orientation towards political revolution and in the practice that follows from it, this dichotomy does not disappear: the way of life of people remains unchanged. Therefore it is not surprising that after the conquest of political power the mass base gets thinner and thinner, and disappears altogether. The majority of the population turns back to the bourgeois way of life, and a minority is fossilised in an alienated citizen-existence. To quote Engels: the realm of reason is transformed into the realm of the bourgeoisie.

(4) *Total revolutionary practice.* This fourth type of practice also includes *revolution in the way of life.* If there is a revolution in the way of life, the mass base of the movement extends permanently. Practice involves wider and wider sections of the population in the movement, and the everyday life of people undergoes a transformation precisely because of their involvement. That is why a revolution in the way of life is always irreversible within a foreseeable historical period. Revolution in the way of life is exemplified in the European history of christianity and, in the case of certain countries, in the Renaissance.

However, while I am saying that total social revolutions include revolutions in the way of life, I am not saying at the same time that revolutions in the way of life invariably involve total social revolutions. On the contrary, we can be sure that in history there has not yet existed the kind of re-

64

volution in the way of life which was, simultaneously, a consciously intended total social revolution embracing the economy, the political sphere and culture.

But when Marx wrote about the communist movement, he had in mind a total revolutionary practice of this kind. His conception was of course not founded on historical analogies. As the proletarian movement matures on the terrain of bourgeois society, it inevitably contains the element of political revolution, i.e. the necessity of conquering political power. But for Marx, the political revolution is only one of the stages, and human emancipation becomes counterposed to political emancipation. It is not possible here to go more deeply into this problem. We can only make the point that the total social revolution projected by Marx presupposes, right from the very first phases of the development of the movement, the *transcendence of the bourgeois structure of theory and practice*. All three kinds of practice analysed above — partial reforms, general reform, and the movements of political revolution — are based on a structure of theory and practice which belongs to bourgeois commodity-production.

Let us inquire how, in the first three cases, the "theoretical product" comes to be purchased, how its realisation or attempted realisation is carried out, and for what motives.

A growing demand for a certain "theoretical product" manifests the *need* for it. And this circumstance — if we leave aside the plain consumption of culture — manifests the fact that the social theory in question has grasped and formulated an existing (and not only theoretically supposed) need.

If we follow this through, we inevitably have to analyse the concept of "social need", especially since the concept of "need", though frequently used, is indeterminate, very vague and altogether empirical.

Need is a conscious desire, aspiration, intention, always directed towards a certain object, and as such it motivates action. The object in question is a *social* product; it does not matter whether it is a commodity, a way of life, or "another person", etc. Social objectivation and need are correlated to each other: the former fixes the "framework" of the needs of individuals who belong to a certain social stratum in a given

65

society. For needs are always individual (since only human beings can consciously desire, aspire or intend) and at the same time social (since all the needs are already "offered" in the social objectivations). "Natural needs" do not exist. For example, air is not an object of need, but a condition of our existence, though the fact that we prefer fresh, clean air to polluted air is already itself a need. All the same, we must also distinguish between the so-called "existential needs" or "conditions of life" and properly "human needs".

"Existential needs" or "conditions of life" are ontologically primary, being founded on the instinct of self-preservation. They consist, amongst other things, of the need for nourishment, sexual need, the need for social contact and co-operation, the need for activity. Even these needs cannot be defined as "natural", since in their concrete forms — as needs proper — they are interpretable only within a certain social context. Not even the need for nourishment can be defined with "biological precision". It is enough to note, for example, the fact that in certain African communities the calorie diet has remained considerably below the minimum regarded as indispensable for survival, and yet they were not undernourished from the point of view of maintaining their social homeostasis. Undernourishment has developed solely as an effect of a disturbance of the social equilibrium. We can state, in general, that satisfaction of existential needs at a given level is guaranteed by the structure of the primitive societies. The limit of that satisfaction is nature: mass death through famine is the consequence of natural catastrophes. Capitalism is the first society that by its social structure condemns entire classes of the population to struggle daily to satisfy their purely existential needs, from the time of the primitive accumulation of capital up to twentieth-century Europe, and up to the present day in the Third World. In this sense Marx speaks of the working class of his time as a class "without needs", that is, reduced to an animal level in the satisfaction of its existential needs.

In contrast to the "conditions of life", the "human needs" proper are directed towards objects, the desire for which is not motivated by natural drives. They consist, for example, of

66

more recreation than is necessary for the reproduction of labour power, cultural activity, adult play, meditation, friendship, love, self-realisation in the objectivations, moral needs. They also consist of the alienated human needs, such as money, power, possession. With the development of capitalism, in parallel to the restriction imposed upon the working class to struggle for the satisfaction of its purely existential needs, the alienated needs have obtained a position of dominance. The only change one can see in modern capitalist society (at least in Europe and North America) is that the dominance of alienated human needs reaches wider and wider strata, including the working class as well.

Non-alienated human needs have a *qualitative* character. Their development is not distinguished by a practically infinite accumulation of objects that serve to satisfy needs, but by their growing many-sidedness, which Marx calls their "wealth". I should remark at this point that the distinction between the existential needs and the non-alienated human needs is relative. The non-alienated human needs can absorb certain existential needs under certain conditions: take, for example, the mutual need of men and women for each other.

Alienated needs, however, have a *quantitative* character. The process of their accumulation is practically infinite. If we take purely quantitative needs into consideration, it is difficult to find the point at which they reach "saturation level". The infinite accumulation of quantitative (alienated) needs can be hindered only by the emergence and dominance of qualitative needs. From this point of view, there is no ambiguity in the conception that Marx had of communism: it is the social process that realises the ever-expanding domination of qualitative (non-alienated) human needs over the existential and alienated (quantitative) human needs.

Having completed this necessary digression, we can return to the various types of theory and practice. As I have already said, the practical efficacy of a theory depends upon its ability to "palpate" real needs. But why do needs have to be "palpated"?

The needs of the people in a given society are "offered" by the concrete and current objectivations of that society. The

67

objectivations demarcate the limits of the dynamic of needs. After all, this is also true for capitalism, even if in capitalist society the interaction between needs and objectivations is far more complex than that of the preceding non-"pure" societies.

We have already seen one of the reasons behind this: the simple accumulation of purely quantitative needs assumed a radically dominant role from early capitalism on. In its turn, this is itself the consequence of a factor that acts at a deeper level: capitalism is the first essentially dynamic society, in which not only the sum total of available consumer goods increases, by means of an incredible acceleration of the rhythm of production, but also new goods and new kinds of goods are continually invented, and in consequence the needs for them as well. Furthermore, capitalism is the first "open" society, in which needs — in the given objectivations — are not "reserved" to a particular social class or stratum. If the object of a need takes its place among the objectivations, it can become, at least in theory, a need for everyone, regardless of whether everyone *de facto* possesses the means of satisfying the need in question. This is true for all kinds of need, and not only for those which are quantitative. So not only is one integrated structure of needs "offered" by a relatively homogeneous system of objectivations, and consequently of values, but at least in theory, one can choose from among the needs "offered" by heterogeneous objectivations. Thus the formation of different personal hierarchies of needs becomes possible. Furthermore, capitalist society is the first one that is not based on organic communities; the only "community" in it is the commodity relation. In earlier societies the value-hierarchy of needs evolved within the community, and the individual more or less accepted the values of needs established for him by the community. Once capitalism has asserted itself, this is no longer possible — from this point of view, something relatively direct is substituted for a manifold system of mediations.

A member of the community was not constrained to "palpate" needs. He was simply *aware* of the needs of the members of his community and — if he had a certain theoretical capacity — he could express them, at different levels, with maybe more or less profundity and more or less coherence. When he expressed the needs of another community, he was able to base himself on needs that had already been articulated in one community. This is the case in Thomas Aquinas and in Plato as well. But in capitalist society, where organic community does not exist, the theoretician — as intellectual worker — is subject, to an ever greater extent, to the division of labour, and therefore a similar direct expression of needs based upon stable objectivations is no longer possible. The theoretician is thus compelled to visualise the structure of society and to elaborate his theory from his own individual viewpoint, and only *post festum* — on the market — will it be clear whether he has succeeded in palpating real needs, that is in expressing, consciously or spontaneously, such kinds of needs in his theory. Furthermore, since needs are "offered" by heterogeneous objectivations, the terrain of theoretical choice gets larger and larger, at least in principle.

A conscious *choice of values* (in this case: the personal hierarchy of values, or preference for certain needs rather than others, preference for the needs of certain classes against those of others) will play a decisive role in whether the theory will be purchased or not, whether it will be applied or not and, if it is applied, what social class or social strata will apply it. Insight into the social structure, especially when it is deep and many-sided, can lead to the paradoxical result that no social stratum recognises in the theory in question the expression of its own needs, not even in cases where in reality the theory corresponds to such a stratum. This was the fate of Hobbes's *Leviathan* (among others). It can lead also to situations that are no less paradoxical, for example when certain aspects of the theory are transformed into practice and penetrate the masses (since they correspond to their urgent and fundamental needs) while the totality of the theory remains outside of that process. This has been the fate of marxism from the end of the nineteenth century onwards: for, from the rise of capitalism onwards, the quantitative "human needs" and purely existential needs degraded into quantitative needs have become dominant, and therefore it is precisely those theories (or aspects of theories) which express these quantitative and purely existential needs or appeal to them which find their way most rapidly

69

into practice.

I shall now try to summarise the relationship that links the four types of practice that have been analysed to the various types of need and to the theories that express them.

The theories and movements of partial reform are generally linked to needs that have already been articulated, formulated and expressed, and their objective is to satisfy or to channel these needs. In most cases their function is — consciously or unconsciously — to siphon off discontent, or to eliminate the social malfunctions manifested in the discontent of certain social classes or strata. They always appeal to existential or quantitative needs, but only if they have already become manifest, whether spontaneously or otherwise. Therefore, if it remains isolated, this type of theory is going to be organically integrated with the defence of the given society and with the practice which keeps it working. In this case the relationship between theory and practice (the "think-tank" model is only the last phase of it) conforms to the structure of commodity production. If there is a demand for a theory of partial reform, it is always effective demand: that is, it does or may have the appropriate material background and means of power to satisfy the requirements of the theory.

The theories of general reform are equally linked to means which are manifest and articulated, but not in a direct way. By the general formulation of these needs, the movements and propaganda activities of these theories — that is, their specific objectivations — "provide" a large number of people with needs that hitherto were not present in their lives, people who were not up to that point conscious of the grounds of their discontent and dissatisfaction. These same objectivations, precisely because they raise the question of transforming the whole of society, can mediate new needs too. However, these new needs do not constitute an integrated, organic structure. The theory exercises its role as a mobiliser by formulating the contradiction between needs and the existence of the class (or stratum), the contradiction between needs and the failure to satisfy them. The needs to which this theory appeals are first of all existential needs, and only secondarily quantitative or certain qualitative needs. The relationship between theory and

70

practice in this case conforms overall to the structure of commodity production (the "think tank" has no function in movements of this kind). The increase and expansion of demand tends more or less to assimilate the theory and to condition it mainly to satisfy existential and quantitative needs. The capitalist structure of theory and practice is not transcended. That is why movements of this kind show an affinity with the first model of theory and practice. The original idea of general reform is eclipsed behind direct action for the execution of partial reform. As I have already said, this was the typical career of the social democratic movements at the turn of the century.

The political revolutionary theories and movements, being based upon the modern separation between the bourgeois and the citizen, display their intrinsic dualism in the formulation of needs too. They make no efforts to raise the masses, through the movement, beyond the level of needs "offered" by bourgeois society. The mobilisation of the masses is based upon the structure of needs developed by bourgeois society. Great emphasis all the same is placed upon the mobilisation of passions, as the target aimed at is a rapid and radical transformation. But the passions set in motion (at least in mass dimensions) can only be those that have been formed and developed within bourgeois society. This very fact — the appeal to needs and passions developed within bourgeois society — is one of the decisive factors giving rise to the typical process that we have seen above: the ebbing of the mass movement after the conquest of political power. On the other hand, it is well-known that the leading force of the political revolutionary movement is the citizen élite. The élite can maintain its capacity for action only by consciously renouncing the satisfaction of a part of its own (existential and quantitative) needs, at least for the time being. This sacrifice — revolutionary asceticism — can initiate the most heroic actions, which deserve the admiration of people. The objectivations of revolutionary political practice imply the transformation of the hierarchy of needs, but this transformation has its disadvantages. In the first place the double standard does not overcome but, on the contrary, reinforces the contradictions between bourgeois and citizen. Secondly, the system of needs developed in bourgeois society remains intact — at least in the last analysis — in the case of the citizen too, with the sole difference that the satisfaction of his needs is projected into the future. And last but not least, the aim of transforming the hierarchy of needs is very effective in appealing to one of the quantitative needs dominant in bourgeois society: the need for power. That is why the asceticism of the élite cannot overcome alienation, and why, furthermore, in spite of its own heroism, it in fact preserves it.

Everything serves to show that even the political revolutionary movements do not basically transform the structure of the relationship between theory and practice in bourgeois society. Theory is based once again on existing needs, and if it tries to develop new needs — even qualitative ones — the attempt remains as accidental as in the movements of general reform. This theory is incapable of elaborating an integrated structure of preference either. It is condemned — both in the mass movement and in the élite — to conform to needs that have already been developed within capitalist society, even if the forms are undergoing a change. The fate of the Jacobin ideology is a striking and classical example of this pattern. This is why political revolutions do not give rise to irreversible modifications in the daily life and in the system of needs of the masses.

Movements for total social revolution cannot either be formed or gain their "victory" in this way. I have put the word victory in inverted commas because the victory of total revolutionary movements cannot be fixed at some definite point in time. It is not an act or a complex of acts, but is invariably a process. It is a process whose vehicle is the people, on an even wider scale. In total revolutionary movements, people themselves transform their own structure of needs and values, in the permanent sequence of objectivations. Here theory does not "conform" to the existing needs of the masses, needs already formed or in the process of formation, it does not appeal to the contradiction between needs and existence, but develops and takes shape in the organised — structured — mass movements themselves. Revolution, in the sense in which Marx

72

meant the word, is a total social revolution that therefore presupposes or implies overcoming the structure of the relationship between theory and practice in bourgeois society, and the capitalist structure of needs in its totality.

This explains why the realisation of Marx's theory is such a complex matter. The total social revolution must be developed in a society whose structure is based upon commodity production and the division of labour, and in which, as a result, the relationship between theory and practice has emerged as a general problem and has been realised by the mediation of the market as a general practice. A universal restructuring of needs and values has to be realised in a society in which alienation is omnipresent, even if the working class "feels uncomfortable" within its framework; a society in which the needs of the masses are pre-eminently either existential or quantitative. In order to attain to these objectives, political revolution is obviously necessary, but by itself it is incapable of realising this radically new structure. Marx repeatedly tried to resolve this dilemma, first of all by means of the concept of "radical needs". The needs of the working class are "radical", since it is the class whose needs cannot be satisfied within the framework of bourgeois society, for a reason of principle: the satisfaction of the needs of this class necessarily transcends the whole structure of bourgeois society, and consequently the structure of needs as well. The working class can free itself only if at the same time it frees mankind, if it initiates a social dynamic that leads to the positive abolition of private property and the elimination of alienation. But the real problem comes when we realise that the "radical needs" are not proper needs in the everyday meaning of the word. They are not needs that exist, and they are not "extensions" of needs that exist, because they presuppose a working class which has developed a consciousness of its own historical mission (an "imputed consciousness", in the words of Georg Lukács), and which decides and acts according to it. Thus, by analogy, we can call "radical needs" "imputed needs". However, historical experience up to the present has demonstrated that without and end to the bourgeois way of life and the bourgeois structure, this kind of "imputed consciousness" does not develop in the masses, and consequently "radical needs" do not develop either. It is their appreciation of this situation, and not the "falsification" of Marx's doctrine, that has led the various tendencies of the working-class movement to appeal to existing needs (needs which have already formed or are in process of formation in bourgeois society), and chiefly to existential and quantitative needs.

If we take seriously Marx's programme of a total social revolution, we must open new paths, precisely because of the lesson history teaches us. The path must be total revolution in the way of life, and through this the formation of new life-styles and new structures of need, which penetrate the lives of people from everyday life to the most complicated human activities. It is only people who consciously organise themselves in communities who can carry through the formation of this new structure of needs. But if the "radical needs" are not proper needs at all before this stage, does there exist any real basis for organising such communities? Is this kind of programme not a utopia?

I am convinced that the conditions of such a programme have already developed; they can be deciphered in the behaviour of ever broader sections of the population. Indeed, it may be said that ever broader masses of human beings are unsatisfied, feel lost in the world of quantitative needs, and are therefore spontaneously seeking a form of life in which quantitative needs are not dominant. Many groups of young people in the most developed industrial societies, and the best of them, abandon the refrigerator, car, and prestige-values of their parents; masses of students, again the best, abandon the universities for similar reasons; new family structures proliferate, assuming the form of communes. All this manifests the rise of the need to transform the existing structure of needs. Whatever the nature of these qualitative needs which hinder the quantitative ones, they indicate that a community movement which develops radical needs is no longer, at least not necessarily, a utopia.

Obviously, the total social revolution — if it is to be realised — does not negate but preserves the activity for partial reform, general reform and political revolution as elements, though as means rather than as final aims. It falls to the socialist movement to develop communities, embracing ever broader masses, in which needs come to be restructured under the dominance of qualitative needs. Only a movement of this kind is capable of eliminating the dualism between educator and educated, élite and mass, citizen and bourgeois, theory and practice, which have all developed within bourgeois society.

What would be the structural relationship of theory and practice in a total social revolution? As it would consist of organic communities, distinguished from the old types of community by the fact that they would be based on free personal choice, it is no longer the "market" where theory and practice meet. There would be the communities themselves — their aspirations and needs — to produce theory, expressing and formulating these aspirations and these needs more or less adequately, more or less profoundly and coherently, and the communities themselves would constantly control and correct this theory through the mediation of their own activity, in which the activity of the theoretician would constitute an organic part. Theory would arise organically from everyday practice; this obviously does not mean that theory cannot correct or control the practice that produces it. But it would not be simply a question of theory exercising its influence on practice, but of the practice and the corresponding theory of one community influencing the theory and practice of the others. So the general problem of theory and practice — which is, as we have seen, the particular problem of bourgeois society — would lose its validity.

5
Maria Markus

WOMEN AND WORK: EMANCIPATION AT A DEAD END

Throughout history and in virtually every society, there have existed inequalities between men and women; however, it was only during the development of Western industrialised society that this fact actually became a social problem and the basis for a social movement. I can here mention only two of the major factors of the many and complex ones that contributed to the development of the "women problem".

One of these factors is that the developing bourgeois society, with its growing middle class, placed emphasis on equality as one of its fundamental credos — formal legal and political equality, at any rate. However, though certain traditional aspects of the position of women consequently became social anomalies in the context of the new, widely accepted system of values, they did continue to exist.

The second factor is that, with the growth of industrialisation, the economic role of women changed. Previously, in agrarian-based societies, the family was both the basic cell of society and also the basic unit of economic production; the man and the woman both produced goods within the confines of the family, mainly for consumption within the family but also for sale or exchange. For example, the woman in addition to being the homemaker wove clothes, made candles, helped in rearing the livestock, and so on. And although a woman's labour was not rated as high in value as that of a man, she was all the same an economic producer and enjoyed some of the independence and dignity of that status.

However, all this gradually changed as bourgeois society developed and specialisation increased— characterised by such

76

things as movement into towns, the growth of the guilds, the development of commercial enterprises and a strong business class, and then industrialisation. Where the production of goods had once taken place primarily within the family circle, it now moved outside the home and into factories and workshops. Men, too, moved outside the home and continued as direct economic producers. Women, however, remained behind, no longer as economic producers but as the breeders and raisers of children, doing domestic chores. What this meant was that the existing sexual dualism took on an added economic slant, and the manifestation of this was the concrete fact that women became totally dependent economically on male "breadwinners".

Precisely because social injustice to women was grounded in this strong economic dependence, the feminist movements which arose in the nineteenth century to struggle for women's emancipation demanded not only political and legal equality but also the right to work. This demand coincided with, on the one hand, the need for cheap unskilled labour within the burgeoning industrial society, and, on the other hand, the need of the poorest families to supplement inadequate incomes.

The right of women to work, however, was not regarded by the women's movement as a question of financial liberation alone, but also as the foundation which would enable women to exercise the human right of choosing and living the kind of life they wanted. Those movements which were inspired by marxism in particular emphasised this demand, since according to their ideology work is a fundamental way of ensuring the development and fulfilment of the human character.

The impasse

In spite of everything, the matter of work is precisely the area in which a dead end has to some extent been reached in women's emancipation in the developed and semi-developed industrial countries (which are the ones under discussion here).

It can generally be said that in both capitalist and socialist countries, as far as formal equality is concerned — political and legal equality — the primary objectives of the fight for

77

emancipation have been achieved, although in almost every country there are still a number of unsolved problems and inequalities which are legally endorsed. The employment figures are an indication that there has been some quite impressive progress; there can be no doubt that today more women work, more women occupy positions of importance in economic and in public life, more women are receiving education than ever before.

Notwithstanding this, the changes in this area tend to be mainly in terms of increased numbers, as can be seen from a rough analysis of the relevant data, and do not show any significant alteration in the condition of women. Nor do they even provide hope that the near future will see the problem of inequality solved.

What makes the situation worse is that although there are women's organisations in every country, the intensity of the struggle for the emancipation of women has considerably lessened in comparison with the situation at the end of the last century and the early years of this century. A decisive majority of women, it seems, accept the present situation in which they are far from equal, maybe simply because there seems to be no available alternative.

In a sense women remain as they have always been, instruments in nearly all spheres of life: instruments that will ensure that the population is replenished and children are brought up, instruments to serve the needs of the household and the sexual satisfaction of men, and last but not least instruments that fill the national economy's variable needs for low-grade labour.

I must point out that whatever the social system — be it capitalist or socialist — the current contradictions and dilemmas concerning women's emancipation are in many respects the same. This is in spite of the fact in socialist countries measures have been instituted in various fields (nurseries, kindergartens and day-boarding institutions, subsidised by the state or by enterprises; laws which protect the interests of working mothers, and so on) which arguably provide a better chance for full emancipation, if efforts to maximise efficiency and efforts to ensure a more humane and democratic way of life can be more closely harmonised in these countries.

78

Today, outside the Third World, about one in every three women is gainfully employed. It has become a general rule for unmarried women to take a job, except in certain traditional peasant communities where there are fewer opportunities for employment. The type of woman who stays home doing nothing in between leaving school and getting married is definitely dying out. Similarly, the proportion of working women among those who are married and have families is also increasing everywhere throughout the world. This generally favourable picture changes significantly, however, when we look at the occupational and employment structure of the female labour force.

The relevant data show clearly that women work not as the equals of men but as a less qualified, cheaper labour force, generally under worse conditions and doing the least interesting jobs. Thus, according to the figures for 1960, while 35 per cent of all those employed in Hungary were women, they made up only 20 per cent of all executives and professionals, and only 15 per cent of skilled workers. However, 56 per cent of lower grade administrative and commercial employees, 43 per cent of semi-skilled and 42 per cent of unskilled workers were women.

Connected with the generally lower working status of women is the fact that when they do highly trained work it is often in fields and professions which are low in social prestige. There are two striking aspects to this state of affairs. The first is the tendency — to be observed in almost all countries — for certain professions of high prestige and income to go down significantly in prestige and relatively in income as soon as women take them over. The second aspect is the corollary of the first: it is only when certain professions have started to decline in prestige and relative income, as a result of certain social and economic processes, that women are able to enter these professions in any large numbers. For example, this is generally true of the teaching profession, and in some countries a similar tendency can be seen in connection with pharmacy and certain branches of medical practice.

There is a serious discrepancy even in these professions between the total number of women involved and those in positions of responsibility. In the USA 86 per cent of primary school teachers are women, yet only 50 per cent of primary schools are run by headmistresses; only 9 per cent of secondary schools are headed by women. In Poland 10 per cent of the women who teach in a general school carry out the duties of a head, as against 40 per cent of the male teachers.

From the above facts it follows that the average income of women is well below that of men; and this is reinforced by the well-known fact that very often women do not get the same pay as men doing the same work. You hear this sort of discrimination justified less and less these days by the argument that women are not capable of work that demands a high level of specialised knowledge and an ability to take decisions and give directions — though in some places such views still survive. One is more likely to hear the argument that women are not a stable and reliable workforce, because of their role as child-bearers and child-rearers with household duties that do not allow them to put as much thought and energy into their employment as men do; therefore, it is argued, their work cannot from the viewpoint of practical economics be equal in value to that of men.

It cannot be denied that in present circumstances there is some justification for this point of view. And what lends it further support is the widespread general attitude that all women, regardless of their individual talents and interests, are by their biological characteristics destined for a role which at least for a protracted length of time necessarily disables them from carrying out any other social role with the requisite energy.

Women's "second shift"

These are the facts and ideas that have brought about the well-known problem of the "second shift" — where a woman works one shift in office or factory, and then works a second shift at home doing the household and child-care chores that are considered especially hers. It is precisely this currently insoluble problem of the double shift which largely explains why the drive for female emancipation is currently at a standstill; it is precisely this which has betrayed the high expectations of the traditional feminist movements.

Let us consider some current facts and figures which show how time-consuming household duties are. Myrdal and Klein quote calculations showing that while the whole of Swedish industry uses only 1,290 million working hours annually, 2,340 million hours are spent annually in Sweden on shopping, preparing meals and washing up.

TABLE 1. *Hours spent daily on work in the home*

Country	Men			Working women			Non-working women		
	Married	Un-married	Av.	Married	Un-married	Av.	Married	Un-married	Av.
Belgium	0.6	0.4	0.6	3.3	1.5	2.7	6.0	3.4	5.6
Czechoslovakia	1.5	1.1	1.5	4.3	3.0	4.1	6.1	4.6	5.8
France	1.2	0.9	1.2	3.7	2.4	3.1	5.8	2.5	5.5
Federal Republic of Germany	1.1	0.8	1.1	4.5	2.3	3.6	6.3	4.6	6.0
Hungary	1.5	0.8	1.3	4.3	2.4	3.8	8.0	5.4	7.7
Poland	1.2	0.4	1.0	3.6	2.1	3.0	6.4	4.0	5.9
USSR	1.1	0.7	1.0	3.5	2.4	3.1	6.3	3.4	4.7
United States	0.6	0.5	0.6	3.2	1.9	2.6	5.1	3.8	5.1

Table 1 (based on an international comparative study carried out by the Vienna Institute of Social Studies) shows the average number of hours spent daily on household duties in various countries by men and women. These data do not include time spent with children, or on shopping, which would generally increase the figures given here by at least one hour a day in the case of married women holding jobs.

According to the ideologies of the traditional feminist movements, household duties should be "socialised" — largely taken over by service establishments provided by the society, as private or public enterprises. It was held that this, and a more equitable distribution of the remaining household chores among all members of the family, would allow women to play their part in the world of employment as equals, with the full opportunity to choose the way of life best suited to their personalities, interests and abilities. That these hopes were not very realistic is proved by the figures in Table 1, as well as by everyday

81

experience; for whether married or not, working or not, all women still put in far more time on household chores than men. Additional proof is to be found in data showing that women in large cities on average spend more time on household duties than village women; one would have thought that the greater availability of services and of domestic appliances would make the reverse the case.

It could be argued that two factors played a part in arresting the "socialisation" of household duties to the desired extent. One of them is economic: the cost of the services concerned, in view of the fact that they are only moderately mechanised, has become relatively high, with the rise in wages and with spreading industrialisation. So if women, particularly those with low qualifications and low income — in other words the decisive majority — want to use paid services (restaurants, laundries, etc.) in place of their own work in the household, their own incomes are not sufficient to cover the costs. As a result, a vicious circle is formed. The low-paid work done by women does not allow them to free themselves from any significant part of their household duties; but on the other hand the burden of the "second shift" prevents them from being able to improve their qualifications in order to do better-paid work.

In itself, however, this economic reason is insufficient; for in a significant proportion of the families in the high-income bracket the wife still does a disproportionate amount of the housework herself, regardless of the technical and financial possibilities that exist. Even among highly qualified women a large proportion (varying from country to country) give up their professions either temporarily or permanently, particularly after the birth of a child. Another very fundamental and general factor is involved, it seems, apart from the question of bringing up children.

The performance of household routines and functions is intimately connected with the personal lives of the members of the family. Their lives are organised with the home as the centre, around which highly individualised activities — eating, relaxing, etc. — are carried out. Impersonal, purely functional relationships put considerable strain on each individual in

modern society, and frequently there is a danger of depersonali-
sation. So it is understandable that there is a spontaneous resistance to the household being socialised by the removal of any
function at present associated with it, and a defence of the
individuality of the home — and this is at the expense of the
woman. Although it is hard to prove with data, everyday observation indeed suggests that this resistance is greatest in those
strata of society whose members have least opportunity for
expressing their personalities freely and creatively beyond the
walls of the home.

Reconciling home and employment: two trends

It is possible today to distinguish two well-differentiated trends
for reconciling the joint realities of the modern woman's life,
which consist in holding a job outside the home as well as
continuing the tradition of being a housewife and the bearer
and rearer of children. One trend is typified by the pattern
which over the past ten years or so has been established in the
USA; the other by the pattern which exists in the socialist
countries (although not only there). Each trend has advantages
and disadvantages; neither provides an ideal solution for the
problem.

What characterises the North American pattern is that a girl
works until marriage, or until the birth of her first child, then
withdraws from her employment; she then takes up a job
again ten or twenty years later when her children are no longer
small. In the socialist countries, however, the pattern is that
the majority of working women remain employed until they
retire, and in order to help them do this they receive various
aids and concessions from the state and from the enterprises
where they work during the child-raising period.

Figure 2 shows how these two patterns differently affect the
proportion of women who work.

For the socialist pattern (as typified by Hungary), the proportion of working women stays relatively constant for all age
groups, with a very gradual decline over the years from the
peak in the group aged twenty to twenty-four. On the other
hand, in the North American pattern there is a relatively sharp

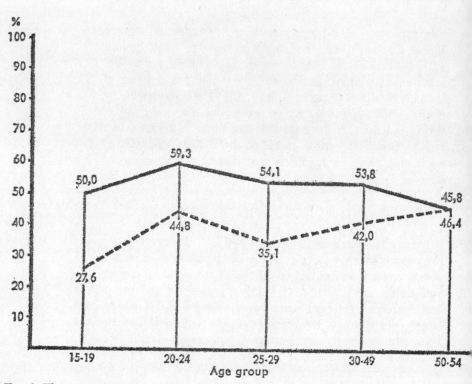

%

FIG. 2. The proportion of working women in different age groups in Hungary (———) and the United States (– – – –).

drop in the proportion of working women between the twenty-to-twenty-four and twenty-five-to-twenty-nine age groups, followed by a gradual increase over succeeding age groups as women resume paid employment when their children no longer need close care.

Many enlightened supporters of women's equality hope that the spread of the North American trend will provide a definite solution to the problem of the double shift for women. It is pointed out that the average life-span of women has greatly increased, that there has been a considerable decline in the number of children in an average family, and that being a full-time mother therefore involves no more than about fifteen years of a womans' life nowadays. Women may have another twenty years to devote to their "second careers", which might be either in the profession in which they were originally trained and perhaps worked, or a different one.

Undoubtedly, the North American model does have certain attractive features in today's circumstances, and not just from the viewpoint of the children, who certainly, during their early years, need close relationships with specific adults, relationships which generally the family is better at providing than the best nursery. From the point of view of women as well it has positive values: they are relieved of the double burden at a time when home responsibilities are at their heaviest.

Yet obviously this absence of fifteen years, or even less, from paid employment outside the home automatically disqualifies women from parity with men in this sphere, since it is during the most active and productive period of their lives that they withdraw from it. The fast pace of technological and scientific progress rapidly leaves behind anyone who does not keep abreast by everyday practice. Thus the prolonged withdrawal from paid employment naturally perpetuates the current state of affairs, where the work that requires the lowest qualifications and consequently is the least creative, most monotonous and worst-paid, is done by women.

To maintain that this is an unsatisfactory situation does not indicate that one holds with the naive view that would identify female emancipation with the abolition of all differences between the sexes, nor that one subscribes to a particular "myth" that paid work is a be-all and end-all. On the contrary, to accept this state of affairs is to reconcile oneself to accepting that women *a priori*, because of their biology, must always have fewer alternatives to choose from than do men. Moreover, so long as personal independence has as its chief basis — or at least one of its chief bases — gainful employment, then this situation preserves the traditional economic dependence of married women on their husbands.

Nor does this seem an acceptable situation from another point of view. Women who withdraw behind the family walls for an extended period of time considerably narrow their opportunities for establishing contacts with other people outside the family circle; it is not necessary to go into details about the negative effects this has on the personalities of

85

such women. However, this fact has wider repercussions at the same time. A family whose life is organised by a woman who is excluded from a larger circle of human relationships, who is to a great extent cut off from most of society and is often therefore no longer interested in it, has a narrowly conservative character in many respects.

This limiting of the scope of women's interests, it can be argued, plays a part in certain crisis phenomena of modern family life, particularly in the growing conflicts between the generations. Only appropriate studies can show whether perhaps the fact that a mother remains at home for a prolonged period, although at first advantageous for a child's early development, may not later be paid for in adolescence. (And similarly, the burden of the "second shift" so thoroughly occupies all a working woman's free time that it can have as restricting an effect as staying at home too long.)

What then of the socialist pattern? It is in theory arguable that in socialist countries the dominant trend (which also corresponds more to the traditional ideas about emancipation) solves the problem in a more positive way since it makes paid employment a permanent feature of a woman's life. However, when the actual situation today is analysed, that assertion cannot be upheld.

As has already been made clear, permanent employment for the great majority of working women today is coupled with the tremendous burden of household responsibilities — which in the socialist countries take up even more time than in the highly developed capitalist countries because the level of technical development and the prevailing standard of living is lower. This is true despite the fact that the state takes important and significant measures to ease this burden, mainly by financing services in connection with child-care. The majority of these women work because of purely economic pressures, and hold low-grade jobs which frequently are more monotonous and subject to worse conditions than average.

Recently certain of the socialist countries have taken steps which may shape women's lives more in the North American mould. For example, in Hungary measures have lately been introduced entitling a woman, after her twenty weeks of mater-

86

nity leave on full pay, to remain at home on leave of absence from her job until her child is three years old. In the case of successive births this period is extended until the youngest child is three. The mother who chooses to stay at home is paid during this time 600 forints a months for each child under the age of three, and the state guarantees that the mother when she returns to work will have employment similar to what she had before bearing the child, and with no loss of rights. These regulations are of particular assistance to women doing low-paid unskilled work, and of course it is mainly these women who take advantage of them. To them — for financial if for no other reasons — home duties are a greater burden than to the average woman.

These measures only came into force in 1967, so it is not yet possible to estimate what long-term effects they will have on the position of women, though the reservations mentioned in connection with the North American model are bound to apply. The long-term effects will, of course, be influenced by the economic and social development of the society itself.

From all the foregoing, it can be said that the movement for the emancipation of women has reached an impasse filled with dilemmas, for which there is no hope of an early solution.

The role of tradition

It should always be borne in mind that the world which women wish to join as equal partners is the world of men, a world in which traditionally the leading and more enterprising roles belong to men. I have dealt above with the subjective reasons for the present stagnation in women's emancipation, and I should now like to point out briefly the influence of traditional attitudes.

Since (to modify Simone de Beauvoir's words) we are not born into but grow into the roles of men or women, the psychology and the attitude of the two sexes are largely determined by the cultural patterns and values which influence this process. The traditional cultural stereotypes which are prejudiced against women have a deep and lasting influence on the "women problem" for the simple reason that their continued acceptance by the majority brings about exactly those results which make them self-justifying and self-perpetuating.

Even in the socialist countries where official marxist ideology is totally in favour of the principle of sexual equality, in actual practice traditional ideas, whereby a woman's main underlying function is to bear and raise children and to keep harmony within the family, still hold sway in public opinion. It may be true enough that schools give the same education to boys and to girls; but the system of values passed on by the education implies approval of the traditional division of labour between the sexes.

The way in which cultural stereotypes persist and dominate is demonstrated by the results of one of our studies conducted with the top class of an elementary school in a working-class area of Budapest. The students in question were about fourteen years old. In this investigation, 87 per cent of the girls mentioned marriage and children as one of their main ambitions. The boys, on the other hand, named as their primary goal in life material success, something to which the girls hardly referred. Only 18 per cent of the boys mentioned forming a family as a primary objective.

Little wonder, then, that it is with the onset of adolescence that there is the most noticeable diminishing of intellectual curiosity in the majority of girls, for their interests are moving in other directions.

New proposals

A woman's organism serves human reproduction. However, the only thing following from this is that women have the human right to bear children; and since this coincides with the interests of society, society must help women to exercise this right.

Offering a number of concessions which will benefit working women, such as those mentioned above, is one possible way of helping. All the same, however generous such arrangements may be, what they are ultimately worth seems to be in doubt since they firmly codify a situation in which women do not have equal value as a workforce.

88

It is for this reason, I believe, that society should not merely apply its efforts to establishing "compensatory" privileges for women who are employed. What society ought above all to do is to create the general conditions to enable large numbers of women to participate equally in every aspect of social life. This obviously calls for a continuing struggle against the prejudices that stand in the way of a more even sharing of the burdens of household work; but it also demands much more than that.

First, regardless of the obstacles a major financial effort must be made to provide a broad range and network of service organisations and establishments to take over a large portion of the household work. The cost of these services should be low enough for all women, whatever their income, to be able to make use of them. Their existence is dependent simply on how much society as a whole is prepared to concentrate its resources in order to establish, maintain and develop them.

It may also be quite possible to "socialise" some aspects of housework in a different way. The dullness of housework today, and the consequently low efficiency and low prestige associated with it, no doubt derives largely from the fact that it is an untrained and unskilled occupation. Might it not be possible to provide training which will turn at least some household activities — such as looking after children — into trades or professions? Certain people could then look after their own homes and do the appropriate work of a few other famiiles at the same time. Thus realistic alternatives would be created both for women who prefer activity within a family environment and for those who want to escape from it.

These proposals are extremely limited; even if they were to be successfully applied the result would be no more than that women would at last become equal members in a world which itself is very far from being emancipated. It is this fact which decisively determines how far the true emancipation of women can go.

For as long as much of the work done by all people is physically burdensome, uninteresting and monotonous, as long as impersonal social mechanisms regulate how various kinds of work are allocated to people irrespective of their wishes and individuality, then women cannot be truly emancipated, for no one is. To paraphrase Marx, female emancipation is not possible without human emancipation, that is without the existence of circumstances in which every man and woman has the chance of choosing an occupation best suited to his or her personality, interests and abilities.

6
Maria Markus and Andras Hegedus

COMMUNITY AND INDIVIDUALITY

One of the current basic problems of social progress is whether the undoubtedly fast development of the productive forces will permit a new way of life to take shape. There are two essential preconditions for this: social conditions that further the growth of personality, and aspirations which will act as an incentive to individuals to make use of the available opportunities and extend their framework. The question is thus whether it is possible to go beyond the objectified individualisation of the consumer society that largely finds its expression in "things", and if so in what way, and whether communal structures oriented towards human values and the development of the individual can take shape.

For Marx the end of private property was not simply the liberation of productive forces and the end of exploitation but precisely the emancipation of the individual from the rule of things, an emancipation which would ensure the growth and development of an authentic human personality.

This way of thinking inevitably links such usually separated notions as community and the individual, and collectivity and individuality. The growth of the personality in Marx's sense cannot be divided from that of social groups which function as communities, which are able to link everyday activities of individuals and larger social units, thus serving to overcome particularity, at least to some extent.*

Community links are not a value in themselves but are the

---

*For the use of the terms "particularity" and "individuality" see Georg Lukács, *Aesthetics*, and Agnes Heller, "Marx's Theory of Revolution and the Revolution in Everyday Life" (in this volume).

necessary field for the development of a harmonious, many-sided and authentic personality. Conditions under which individual lives cannot be arranged without regard for those of others or stand in opposition to them, can only exist within social groups functioning as communities.

Community functions can of course be carried out not only by institutions, organisations and small groups but also by macrostructural units such as nations, social classes, etc., together with their interests, ideologies and value systems. These, however, will not be discussed here, first of all because they would extend the scope of this paper too much, and secondly because in our view that sort of community experience is, as a rule, also transmitted by smaller groups, in which direct personal contact plays a larger role.

Not every such small group truly fulfils community functions, since they are often accidental (i.e. they are not based on a conscious choice of the participants), and what is more they often, by their own nature, strengthen particularity.

From the point of view of community function, the following types of social group can be discerned:

(a) Humanising communities which further the growth of the personality of their members in the sense outlined above, realising the sort of progress beyond particularity which leads towards realisation of man's species-being.

(b) Collectivising communities which serve progressive aims, but which cannot further the growth of personality since they completely subject the individual to the community.

(c) Dehumanising communities which lock and integrate their members into communities whose aim runs counter to the progress of man's species-being, thus producing distorted individuals.

(d) Quasi-communities which appear to be collective but really serve the particularity of their members.

(e) Compensatory communities which provide communal experience in some fringe area, often linked with a hobby.

All these are analytical categories, and in reality never appear in a pure state. Individual social groups need not perform the same function for all their members, and they can change their character in the course of time.

This essay deals with the community functions of various groups in the world of work. This essentially narrows down the subject and concentrates attention on a most important field in the life of modern man. If we bear in mind the fact that traditional community structures based on the family and neighbourhood have lost much of their importance and are largely limited to private life, organisations at the place of work provide the principal framework for the growth of communities. This in no way implies a wish to limit the importance of those theoretical and practical experiments which endeavour to create new communities and ways of life in the private sphere, e.g. by producing new types of family and neighbourhood relations. What we have in mind here are the West German communes or Bjorn Seldens' initiative in creating "large families" based on choice in Scandinavian countries [see *Neues Forum*, 1969]. The same problem in Hungary is discussed in Agnes Heller and Mihaly Vajda, "Family and Communism" (in this volume).

Largely because of the atomisation of life, ways in which man can express and develop his personality must generally be looked for in the world of work, not only directly as part of his working activity, but also in the field of self-management and social control that is connected with it. Besides, man spends most of his time at work, which is a fact that cannot be neglected. A number of sociological investigations have shown that the nature of work and the position in the division of labour largely determine ways of life and aspirations.

The present problems of community life in the workplace are closely linked with the collectives that took shape amongst wage labourers in the first stage of the industrial revolution, of which one of the most significant features is the absorption of the individual in collective communal norms. It differed essentially from the traditionalism of the "naturally given" communities, and was an important step forward, particularly since it was not confined to the same extent to particularities derived from a social "estate" or location. Nevertheless, this still gave little opportunity for the development of individuality.

Modern developments — in industrial societies — pushed this kind of collectivism into the background. The increasingly hierarchical structure at the workplace not only stratified the labour force, but at the same time extended the opportunities for individual advance. As a result, individual objectives relating to social mobility were given a greater importance.

All this has taken place within a framework where the growth of consumer goods and leisure have extended the scope for free choice of a way of life. This is true even where the choice is not between real needs but brands of consumer goods. As Kolakowski has argued: "Petty bourgeois individualism is not the affirmation of personality but its degradation, by producing the sort of apparent personalities whose existence is not linked to activity and production, but to choice amongst finished goods."

This refers primarily to the consumer society, which presumes a relatively high standard of living and a plentiful supply of consumer goods. In societies that have put an end to private ownership of the means of production, once the standard of living begins to rise this appears as one of the most attractive models of development. Its effect is increased by the absence, in theory and practice, of new ways of life that embody socialist values. This does not mean, of course, that these societies have not accumulated the kind of experience whose sociological analysis may help to work out alternatives for the future.

We must begin with a survey of the state of affairs *in statu nascendi*. A peculiar myth of collectivity took shape in the first years of socialism, particularly at the ideological level, which mainly concerned the structure of the workplace. According to this, individual interests and the growth of individual personality must be subordinated to "higher", social, class, enterprise etc. interests, that were often presented as abstractions. Thus what we have termed the "collectivising" community function came to predominate. Two historical circumstances contributed to this. One was the difficulty of the conditions under which socialism came to power. This naturally concentrated attention on the defence of the new system against internal and external opposition, on the struggle against food shortages and last but not least on the primitive accumulation of capital. This necessarily pushed individualisation into the

94

background and made it just about impossible on a larger scale. The second circumstance was that socialism won its first victory in a country where individualisation, which as a mass phenomenon is the product of bourgeois development, was unable to develop because of the underdeveloped social conditions which prevailed in pre-revolutionary Russia, where primitive collectivism still survived in many aspects of life. The model which took shape there was taken over with only slight modifications by European countries, including countries where individualisation had already reached a relatively high level.

Thus the principle of collectivisation became dominant in a form that not only failed to further the development of the individual personality but also described it as being opposed to the common interest. A monolithically interpreted type of socialist man has turned into a principle.

These were all incentives for the growth of collectivising communities of type (b), and not only at places of employment. The housing communes which developed in the Soviet Union straight after the revolution, and were based on the principle of the "equality of poverty", are interesting in this respect. This was repeated in other countries, early on during the transformation period. Such communities generally played a positive role at first. They corresponded to concrete social relations in which homogenising tendencies were the rule. Society had not become hierarchically structured as yet, and many factors counteracted this possible tendency.

The situation changed once a certain degree of stability was achieved. A structurised society took shape in the socialist countries, in which individualisation and individual interests were given an increasingly large role in economics and practical life, though their importance was denied by ideology for some time. Thus "collectivising" communities were not only unable to develop further, they actually regressed, and hierarchical and bureaucratic organisations took their place which generally functioned as "quasi-communities". A typical development in Hungary was the process which transformed the college movement, which was decidedly left-wing and committed to socialism, into student hostels. Similar "progress" took place in many other areas, and thus the contradiction between everyday facts and the proclamation of collective attitudes grew all the time.

A peculiar kind of illusion arose at the same time which presumed that the end of private ownership of the means of production by itself created a satisfactory basis for social integration and for the growth of a communal man, and that this would, so to speak, "automatically" transform organisations at places of work into true communities. Those who support this view consider that communities which further the growth of personality already exist. Anything lacking in this respect, inasmuch as they take notice of it at all, is put down to subjective faults. However, the facts of everyday life do not bear this out but, on the contrary, indicate that there are objective reasons why the problem of community development by organisations at places of work remains unsolved.

The end of private ownership of the means of production has not given the workers' collectives any power of control over the productive process. This has remained the function of various administrative apparatuses of the economic organisations. Under such circumstances work remains wage-labour, in practice the worker sells his labour-power to an administrative institution. This is of course the reason for the quasi-community nature of the enterprise collective, since its basis is a matter of chance for the individual, i.e. of the buying and selling of labour-power, not of free association. The interest of an individual worker is thus expressed by the advantageous selling of his labour-power and not the effective functioning of the institution. The high rate of labour turnover demonstrates this in a telling way.

The new system of management in Hungary promises a change in two directions. On the one hand, collectivist illusions are demolished by making the impossibility of production for direct social needs quite clear, thus offering a practical criticism of the proposition which declares that our society has already overcome wage labour. At the same time, it affords the possibility that a conscious shaping of productive relations will allow the sort of social structures to take shape which will further the growth of real collectivities, at least in certain important fields.

This reform at the same time mobilises certain individualising tendencies which have a positive role in the dynamics of economic development and also in the extension of real opportunities for individual growth. The sort of attitude which completely renounces the principle of collectivism, considering it antiquated, and which wishes to replace it with an individualist system of values and ways of life oriented towards each person's own individual happiness, is a one-sided reflection of this. This is often linked with the nascent managerial-technocratic ideology in socialist countries, which considers collectivism to be an obstacle in the way of economic dynamism and optimisation (and this in spite of the fact that recent research suggests that worker-participation increases performance).

It is, of course, possible that collectivist attitudes will find themselves in opposition to the task of optimisation at certain periods and for a limited time, and that, on the basis of concrete analysis, the latter must be given priority. In the long run, though, commitment to socialism demands the development of the sort of communities which stick to collectivist principles, ensure the growth of individual personality, and serve the purposes of economic dynamism.

The sort of totality and monopoly which was characteristic of traditional pre-capitalist and early working-class communities no longer occurs in these communities, nor are the limits of individual development strictly delimited, without the individual having a chance to change them. An active participation in the shaping of community relations and norms replaces the one-sided subjection of man to communal norms which is the rule in primitive communities. At the same time, the humanising communal functions mentioned in our introduction cannot be limited to the activity of production, but transfuse all aspects of life in some form or other.

The question is whether movements that will result in such humanising communities are likely to appear in the realm of work. This naturally gives rise not only to microstructural (e.g. work organisation) problems, but also to macrostructural ones, since it is in this field that the question of to what extent communities at the workplace will be able to transcend the old forms and framework will be decided.

In order to strengthen such tendencies and allow them to become something that is qualitatively new, the organisation of socialist enterprises must be re-examined, particularly the nature of the wage-labour system. At present, state and even co-operative enterprises and institutions simply buy the worker's labour power and put it at the disposal of the administrative apparatus. As against this, and to the extent that technical conditions permit, one could build on the basis of workers associated in groups, provide them with the means of production, and determine their income on the basis of the labour supplied. The administrative apparatus would exist primarily to serve the interests of such associations.

Modern business management, going right back to Taylor, idealises the break-up of the work process into units which are then reassembled by management experts, without the participation of those doing the work. Changes have lately been carried out in the original Taylor principles, but they do not affect the essence, and are merely devices to lessen the monopoly. Whatever their practical use, they do not change the principle that workers are given partial tasks by others; not only do the teleological functions of determining the objective belong to someone else, but even the way in which the partial process is carried out is not determined by those who actually carry it out. Elton Mayo subjected taylorism to sharp and justified criticism, but even he does not imply essential changes; what he tries to do is to produce community experience at the microstructural level, changing not the conditions but the methods of management. Taylorism has had an influence on socialist society too. In the twenties it seemed the only scientific system of management which appeared rational in the context of the technological level. These methods were further developed in the interests of an increase in productivity, but no one criticised them from the point of view of marxist humanism.

The practical consequence of such marxist criticism would not be a return to the primitive collective spirit which preceded "scientific" labour management, but the growth of communal forms of the sort which were outlined above. One must bear in mind, though, that traditional communities still survive in certain fields of production, and that these are in many cases linked with illusions about their being the embryos of a new collectivism. Organisational forms preserving such primitive collectivism were fairly general in work such as navvying in Hungary, where the worker-collective provided just about the only form of socialising for workers living away from their families. These frequently showed the same norms as their home communities, which only increased their closed nature. This type of community survives to this day without profound changes, in types of work which take people away from their homes such as work in oil-fields, seasonal work on state farms and forests, and also of course navvying.

We had the opportunity to investigate a group of over twenty navvies working in a Transdanubian state farm who all came from one and the same Trans-Tisza village. Its internal structure was relatively homogeneous and strongly patriarchal. The chargehand, who had organised the group himself, had considerable power, without in any way making use of administrative means. The basis of his power was a set of strong collectivist norms which were inhuman and strict in many respects, excluding just about every manifestation of individuality. Sticking to them in closed circumstances nevertheless provided the members of the group with security, and defended them against various influences of the outside world which they did not consider desirable. Group norms determined all their activities, including eating and entertainment. Their wages were saved for their families, they cooked together, their food was poor and traditional, they also entertained each other. Neither party nor trade-union organisations had any influence on them.

The new principles of organisation which have replaced such traditional ones in most places, not only provide no substitute for the communal experience, but polarising the workers, they put them at the mercy of the administration to an even greater extent:

" 'I should like to work in the way', one of the labourers said, 'in which we used to work, at least eight or ten of us together. Not in a large group like this year.' Or another: 'What upsets me is that a man can't chose those he works with, they send someone along and you've

99

got to work with him, that's not right, that has an effect on the shaping of a good collective.' "

The question is whether this dream can be fulfilled by creating the sort of new forms which can transcend primitive communities, new humanising communities which do not conserve the old way of life and which do not hinder the individual in his quest to develop. The other problem is whether such a type of organisation fits into a modern enterprise, and if so then in what form.

Let us look at certain attempts to include this type of organisation (which we shall henceforth call enterprise associations) in more or less modern labour management.

One such attempt was made by brigades of telephone line fitters. This permitted a clash of views concerning these organisational forms to be observed. The type of work demands communal life. The eight to ten members of the brigade spend the whole of the week away from their families in temporary quarters. The time for starting and finishing work is determined, and transport to and from the location is provided by the enterprise. There are work-norms, pay is according to individual performance but cannot exceed average wages. The alternative that the group should undertake the work as an association, see to its food and shelter itself and to work in their own rhythm, without fixed working hours, seemed obvious. Thus continuous supervision and direction would be replaced by acceptance of the completed work.

This alternative looked advantageous from the enterprises's point of view too, since it would have made direction simpler, besides alleviating the shortage of labour. But the trade union made serious objections. One was that the workers, bearing in mind that their pay was low, would exploit their labour-power at the expense of their health, that they would lengthen their working hours and work with greater intensity. Others said that by employing this alternative one could do a week's work in two or three days. At the same time they opposed the idea that the brigade should get money in lieu of food and shelter since they presumed that this would involve a significant drop in standards.

100

Some of these objections are justified in themselves, but they do not touch the essence of the transformation, which would still hold good even if the negative aspects of it were reduced. One might say, to start with, that labour power is exploited to the detriment of health by other types of organisation of labour too, perhaps not in basic official working hours but outside them. A true notion of leisure has not yet taken shape amongst the first generation of workers, and not only for material reasons. Time outside work can only be employed doing nothing, satisfying purely physiological demands; that is why they wish to extend their working hours, especially where poor financial circumstances and special needs are involved, bearing in mind that the demand for differentiated consumption has considerably increased in Hungary in recent years.

In cases like this, workers often try to expend as little energy as possible at their place of work, and employ their strength (often at the expense of their health) in increasing their income outside their proper working hours. The fact that the unofficial price of labour power is double the official one is also a contributing factor. A builder, for example, is paid 12 to 13 forint an hour by state enterprises, and 25 to 30 by small private tradesmen. Discrepancies thus arise between the consumer goods that can be obtained and state and co-operative incomes which give rise not only to the phenomena we have mentioned but also to many kinds of corruption. The association model would encourage processes in which an increase in the intensity of work would permit needs to be largely covered within normal working hours. Though this would not be a barrier in itself to self-exploitation, it is likely to show better results in this respect than the control regulations suggested by the trade unions. A real solution, however, demands the sort of general change which provides other objectives for people than the mere acquisition of worldly goods.

Studying the Szekszard State Farm, we were able to observe the results of many years experience, and also had the benefit of research conducted on the spot by Ferenc Funszabo. The first such groups were organised for work on ploughed land, and that is where they are still operating most successfully. 1,700 to 2,400 yokes of arable land are entrusted to eleven to fourteen men. Not only the land but the necessary machines and chemicals are also at their disposal. The management only controls the execution of previously determined operations. On principle, and lately in practice also, the brigade itself decides what work is done where and by whom, and who is on leave or absent and when. No work-process is measured or standardised by the management: the single standard is the amount produced. They are paid according to the value produced at predetermined rates, a minimum income being guaranteed. The members themselves decide how the income is to be allocated amongst the members of the brigade. The principle is one of equal distribution in proportion to the number of days worked by each. Neither expertise, strength, nor seniority are taken into account. This does not give rise to any special problems, since the groups are relatively homogeneous. Draft contracts are re-negotiated yearly.

The first complex planting brigade was established in 1964; the following year saw another two. By 1967 these three brigades worked three quarters of the planted area. This form of labour organisation is also employed in the vineyards and in animal husbandry, and is beginning to spread to other state farms in the area, which are benefiting from this experience in this type of labour organisation.

There are greater difficulties in industry, where the division of labour is greater and processes are broken down into their parts. As a result, such associations are developing more slowly. The greater individualisation of city life, with the choices it offers, and the internal structure of industry itself, are the two chief sources of the difficulties. The most characteristic feature, besides the division of labour, is a strong hierarchisation. Nevertheless there are endeavours to establish communal forms, though they do not reach the degree discussed above. The most elementary form is the replacement of payment for individual performance by payment for group performance. This creates a group interest and facilitates the development of communities at the place of work.

Conditions are better in industrial development research, where the nature of the work demands that people with a variety of skills co-operate. The teams which are formed there in many ways resemble what we have called enterprise associations. Every research project carried out in this area shows increasing attempts to freely form teams in laboratories and similar places to replace the ones which were previously established in a bureaucratic manner, and attempts too to emancipate them from bureaucratic direction by the enterprises. The strengthening of this tendency is one of the most important contributing factors to the increased efficiency of research and development work. This is borne out both by the surveys conducted and by practical experience. All this allows one to conclude that enterprise associations may well fit in with more advanced types of labour organisation. It is true, though, that these experiments were not prompted by any sort of commitment to collectivist attitudes but by a variety of entrepreneurial interests, such as labour shortages and lack of interest (and therefore lack of efficiency). This is in fact a proof that the time is ripening from a practical point of view too, where the classical type of work and labour organisation will be gradually replaced by a growing number of various types of association amongst workers.

When the socialist brigades were formed the problem was formulated in a more extended way. There was the recognition, to start with, that our society has not given rise to any new way of life. As against previous individual competition, the emphasis was now put on the collective, an emphasis which was interpreted as covering life outside work, too. A number of sociological surveys and a study of brigade logbooks, however, showed that these attempts had largely formal results, that they did not succeed in producing a genuine movement, and that even the brigades which were considered the best often concealed a quasi-community.

In fact the primary objective of the attempts was not to create opportunities for the kind of collectivist association of workers which had a real content, and which workers could freely chose or accept, but to include as large as possible a percentage of workers, even if purely formally, in socialist brigades, or in such as were competing for this title. This was often linked with direct financial incentives: this is particularly demoralising when it is considered that the original idea was that socialist brigades in themselves, without any kind of material incentives, would create more advantageous conditions and a more pleasant way of life.

What also helped to make socialist brigades purely formal was the fact that they were clearly integrated into the hierarchy of the enterprises. The instructions laid down by the Presidium of the Trade Union Council clearly stated that "the leader of brigades competing for the title of socialist brigade will be chosen by the members", but surveys showed that as a rule they are chargehands chosen at a higher level, who as such already have a place in the administrative hierarchy, and who receive a fee for this activity, even though they are not completely relieved of all manual labour.

The fact of inclusion in the official structure is a sufficient obstacle in itself to hinder the enhancement of the associative **and communal character** of the brigades. What we called humanising communities presuppose a certain kind of spontaneity: without it, the movement's character cannot be preserved, and it is necessarily formalised and turned into an organisation.

A movement, in our interpretation, is a continuous struggle for progress beyond the present state of affairs, and for renewal in such a way that the degree of responsibility undertaken by the participants is not determined by their particular interests but by their budding collectivity. Thus their area of movement must be determined by themselves and not from outside.

This kind of humanising community is necessarily linked with the movement for real social control, one of whose main characteristics is that it cannot be and must not become an organisation, since its purpose is not to take over the administration but to place it under the control of the masses. The aim is therefore not some new state of affairs, but the growth of social control as a dynamic process, the production of conditions where men continuously, and not only in the course of a revolutionary situation every now and then, take part in what happens in society and in the determination of their own fate.

Although we have looked primarily at work, we are well aware that all these processes making for collectivisation cannot be divided from society as such, and cannot be realised in one isolated enterprise, or even in one section of the economy. They are an integral part of the reforms which affect society as such, and it is only thus that they can be put into effect in a systematic way.

7
Maria Markus and Andras Hegedus

FREE TIME AND THE DIVISION OF LABOUR

In the works of Marx we can discern the outlines of two conceptions of the possibility for extending human autonomy. Each of these has found its own group of followers, who still exist in the social science thinking of today. According to one conception, the realm of freedom can be attained (given the limitations imposed by the existing division of labour) only *outside* the socially necessary *labour time*. For this reason, the supreme goal of social development is to increase free time and to make use of it in such a way that the individual may avail himself of the material and intellectual wealth of society to an ever growing extent, so that the difference between the stage of development of the individual and the developmental possibilities afforded by society constantly decreases. According to the other conception, the basic task is the humanisation of labour. Therefore fundamental changes must be made *in the sphere of socially necessary labour itself*, first of all by removing the limits created by the division of labour, and then by developing the forms required for real social control. Thus the possibility must be created for each person to realise himself in the world of work.

One of the things which we would like to prove in this study is that the worlds of free time and of work are closely interrelated, and it is therefore impossible to make far-reaching changes in one sphere while leaving the other untouched.

Experience has shown that limiting the attainment of the "realm of freedom" to the time outside work alone is not a solution. The time left free from "official" work is not filled with activities which might serve the fulfilment of the individual and his personality, but is used to make money, in various ways. Thus the activities performed in free time are part of the organisation of production, in various ways, and as a result they are affected by the negative influences of both the division of labour and the existing organisation of work. Both sociological research and experience, disentangled from its illusions, have equally proved that an increase in "free time" does *not*, in itself, change people's way of life but provides, at most, the opportunity to extend existing activities or to introduce new ones which serve to satisfy *the most urgent needs within the given way of life*. The second conception encounters obstacles which are equally great. The division of labour binds people to specific occupations or professions, usually for their entire lives. Furthermore, the choice of these occupations is most frequently determined by external factors beyond the control of the worker himself or herself, and these limitations continue to provide very little possibility for individual development and self-fulfilment. In order to find the way out of this situation, we need to analyse the pitfalls which lie ahead of the two conceptions referred to.

Free time for making money

If we set out from the hopes attached to the increase of free time, one of the most obvious factors (in itself, an unconditionally positive one) is that the amount of time which is "officially" free from work is growing substantially in all the industrially developed countries. This could easily lead us to the conclusion that genuine free time is rising in a similar ratio. In practice, however, in almost all of these countries, the time spent on making money *outside* official working time is also rising substantially. (This is well documented in a book by the Polish sociologist Danecki,[1] which contains data referring to both socialist and capitalist countries. Detailed proof with respect to British workers has been given in a research project under the direction of Zweig.[2]) At present, this is mainly true of men, since owing to the comparatively heavy burden of household work, women indeed have hardly any free time at all. We cannot expect any substantial change in this situation, even if official working time continues to diminish, for it is a well-known fact that mechanisation simply tends to make housework easier rather than to shorten the time required to complete it. Apart from this, the rise in the general level of cultural demands is very time-consuming. Fourastie[3] predicts that in twenty years' time, the number of compulsory working hours in the West will be reduced to thirty, but the time required to perform housework will be some forty to eighty hours, depending on the number of children in the family. At the same time, these household duties are also activities performed under economic pressure (not always to make money, but at any rate to save it), and everything we have said about the forced division of labour applies to them too, regardless of the person involved. (This is not true, of course, for those who freely choose this type of activity.

It is very difficult to determine precisely the magnitude of that part of time which is spent on making money outside "official" work. Various types of activity can be included here, from part-time jobs and overtime, through allotments or housework, to occupations in which people are motivated either by the possibility of supplementary incomes or, at least, by material savings. In many cases people are far better able to identify themselves with their money-earning activities outside their official working time than with their basic jobs, if for no other reason than that in performing this work, they generally have greater independence, since this is usually their own choice. But this does not change the situation. Even if we cannot provide summary data at this point, the results of the various research projects and a good deal of detailed information probably indicate that, alongside the reduction of official working hours, there is an increase (in Hungary too) in the portion of so-called free time spent on "making money", in the broader sense outlined above. According to the most recent sociological surveys concerning the way in which urban industrial wage and salary earners spend their leisure time, seventeen per cent of workers in Budapest heavy industry, fifteen per cent of workers in towns of county status, and twenty-four per cent of those in towns of district status indicated that their overtime had risen. Eighteen per cent of male skilled workers and twenty-six per cent of the professionals in leading positions have *regular* part-time jobs and, in both categories, two-thirds of the workers have *irregular* supplementary employment. The way in which paid holidays are used should also be part of the picture. A substantial part of the workers spend their paid holidays working or, which is likewise not a rare occurrence, do not take their annual leave (or part of it) at all.

As a result, there is very little time left (particularly if we also take into account the growth in social wealth as a whole, and the correspondingly broadening scope of possibilities open to the individual) which, to use Marx's words, is "not absorbed by direct productive work, but [remains] for enjoyment, for leisure, so that it gives scope to free activity and development . . . , which is not determined — as labour is — through the coercion of an external goal that must be executed, the execution of which is 'natural necessity' or, if you prefer, 'social duty'." The question therefore arises: what forces people to spend their free time in money-making activities?

The necessity of working in free time

First of all, we must state that one of these forces is the procuring of the material goods needed for a "respectable standard of living". At the level of development at which Hungary stands today, this is a problem for a comparatively broad layer of people. Of course, when we deal with this consideration it has to be taken into account that the criteria of a "respectable standard of living" have undergone a substantial transformation. Yet it is a fact that certain objects which are considered a part of the elementary conditions of life (for example a flat, or certain other durable consumer goods) cannot be procured from today's average basic wage. This is simply accentuated by the fact that the demand for more free time is overtaken by the growing demand for goods which, although industry is producing them in increasingly large quantities, cannot yet be acquired by great masses of workers because of the given level of the national income. The growth in the "desire for possession" is also influenced by constantly increasing phenomena such as prestige consumption, or even the simple manipulation of demand (for example, through increased advertising, which is aimed at profits).

Both the securing of a "respectable standard of living" and differentiated needs, or even prestige consumption, appear as particularly strong impulses among young people setting up families or becoming independent. They are faced with the necessity of creating the material basis for an independent life (beginning with the flat, progressing through the objects needed for everyday life, and on to supporting an additional person such as a wife or child), and they are also those individuals whose differentiated needs change most dynamically. The endeavour to meet demands of this nature generally interrupts and may even set back the process of cultural development and self-education which school in its best sense had begun. It is precisely in these young age-groups that we can observe extra work and overtime being undertaken most frequently; at the same time, this is where we most frequently find people working in alternating shifts, or on continuous night shift, often at their own request. Although it is mostly during the period of becoming independent and founding families that people are forced to subordinate their lives, including their free time, to making money, this appears as a coercive force in other age-groups too.

The growing material demands of various kinds, and the gap between their quantity and the means available for satisfying them, are not only a source of frustration but undoubtedly also increase the incentive to work for wages. In principle, this ought to provide an opportunity for increasing the tempo of development. But it is difficult to realise this possibility in the sphere of production because the enterprise can only pay higher wages for more or better individual output within rather narrow limits. Greater material advantages can be gained almost exclusively through promotion within the hierarchy. However, not only is this road a restricted one (that is, only a few workers can be promoted, e.g. to a foreman's post), it also has distorted social consequences, since it does not provide any incentive to maximum performance on the job but rather develops standardised models of success, which do not make it possible to take individual talents or skills into

110

account. Some people cannot or perhaps do not want to take this path, and hence their demands (whether they are basic or differentiated) force them to try and achieve greater earnings; the only way they can meet these demands is to use up some of their free time in money-making activities.

The consequences for society

We have tried above to answer the question, what forces people to use their free time to make money? Now we have to look for the mechanism by which the market absorbs the labour thus devoted to it, especially since it seems to happen under conditions which are more favourable to the worker than those which pertain in "official" working time. At the present level of development of society, there is an increasing gap between the population's demand for services and the capacity of the state-owned enterprises and co-operatives to meet these demands. At the same time, there is a constantly growing demand for skilled workers who, outside their official working time, are willing to perform work of this nature, although at a higher price than officially paid. This means that not only is the private sector expanding, but also that there is a rapidly growing number of people undertaking work outside their working hours in both legal forms (with permits) and illegal ones. (This tends to reverse the trend described by Max Weber in which "the factory recruits a very large amount of the skilled labour force from the reserves of small-scale industry, in other words, it allows the latter to train the labour force and then, when training is completed, it withdraws them from there".) In order to enable society to pay for these services, the wages received for "official" work are generally insufficient and, therefore, surplus earnings are needed in some form or other. In the majority of cases, these can only be obtained by sacrificing free time. Thus a peculiar vicious circle develops, for this is the beginning of a process which reproduces its own irrationality on an extended scale. The demand for services not met by the state-owned and co-operative enterprises pushes up the free-market price of labour. In recent years, the free-market price of labour has risen more rapidly

111

than wages in general, and today in many trades it is more than double the official wage level (for example, the official wages of building workers have risen by about twenty-five per cent in the past five years, while the free-market price for workers in this trade has more than doubled).

The reasons for this state of affairs — the higher price level for free-market services, the smaller overheads and taxes, and the far better organised and more intensive work — are comparatively easy to account for, but the evaluation of its consequences is more difficult. One of the most important consequences affects labour intensity. Although it is difficult to prove with quantitative data, it can be logically assumed and supported by everyday experience that the difference between the official and the free-market price of labour plays an important role in the low degree of labour intensity at work. The frequently mentioned slackness of labour discipline is in most cases a conscious restriction of performance, since the worker who receives at work an hourly rate which is half of what he gets for doing the same amount of work during his free time quite naturally reacts by saving his strength. Max Weber described this by saying that "low wages are not identical with cheap labour". For precisely this reason, not all wage rises lead to labour becoming "more expensive" or to such negative consequences as rises in the level of non-regulated prices. However, the picture becomes even more complex: the low degree of labour intensity forces the enterprises to form a labour reserve within the enterprise itself, which enhances the chronic labour shortage. As a result, the state-owned and co-operative enterprises not only try to maintain much larger staffs than justified, but they themselves appear as purchasers of their own workers' free time. It is only in this context that it becomes possible to understand that in spite of all endeavours and all the restrictive measures, neither the extent of overtime nor the ration of part-time and supplementary jobs decreases.

The situation which has developed in the area of overtime is a particularly odd one. In the name of the workers' interests, the trade unions are using all their strength to reduce and even eliminate overtime. At the same time the workers, particularly in trades where there are restricted opportunities for the free-market sale of their labour, consider their incomes acceptable only if the earnings are supplemented with overtime wages. (Zweig, in the work which we have already referred to, mentions an analogous phenomenon in British industry: in his opinion, overtime in sufficient quantities and possibly on a regular basis is one of the permanent demands of the labour force.) In some enterprises the workers themselves create, in an organised way, conditions under which overtime becomes unavoidable. For instance, they are unwilling to carry out certain jobs unless they receive a sufficient quantity of overtime in return. This problem has become manifest with particular clarity in recent years, when the co-operative farms have become centres of attraction for labour not only because they were able to pay higher hourly wages, but also because they were less affected by restrictions on overtime. For reasons which we have already given, this particularly affects the younger workers; today, therefore, we can speak with greater justification of a rising average age-level in certain large metalworking enterprises than in well-run co-operative farms.

The vicious circle which we described earlier includes an almost permanently high rate of labour turnover, and experience has shown that this situation can hardly be changed by administrative measures. To sum up: experience proves that if the reduction of official working hours is not followed by a substantial rise in real wages, and if in addition a demand for true free time does not develop among the social strata involved, then it provides only an illusion of increased freedom. In some way or other, the workers are in fact forced to put their labour on sale in their free time as well.

Free time is turned into a commodity, and this makes it illusory to expect that the self-realisation of man is linked solely to the growth and reorganisation of free time. But this is not the only reason. Sociological research has proved that the specific nature of a job — i.e. its position within the division of labour — determines the entire life of man, including the manner in which he spends his free time. The present forms of the division of labour, however, constitute a serious barrier to the realisation of human autonomy in the sphere of work itself. On the one hand, the majority of workers per-

113

form detail labour which lacks a teleological function from either the vocational or the social point of view. On the other hand, people are tied to a specific vocation and frequently to a specific job for their whole lifetime, almost from childhood until the time they retire and receive their pensions. This is one of the most conservative features of the present organisation of production. A suitable transformation of the organisation of production so as to conform with socialist values would raise two major questions. What changes are necessary in the system of the division of labour? And how can the bonds which we have mentioned be eliminated, or at least loosened?

Without underestimating the importance of the first problem (which we deal with in "Community and Individuality") we should like to concentrate here on the second question, since it is of key importance to the arguments presented in this essay. (This particular essay does not deal with that aspect of the problem which is customarily referred to as the democratisation of social relations, but which we prefer to call the social domination of the producers.)

The allocation of people to the major branches of the social division of labour is today primarily performed by the educational system. It is there that the process begins which results in people being tied for a lifetime to a specific type of work, and possibly to a particular job as well. The school does not prepare the students to form their lives consciously: it merely enables them to fill a narrowly defined occupation or job. Our present school system essentially maps out three patterns of life from the age of fourteen. These not only differ from each other, they are distinctly closed off from each other; they conserve the present social structure and pass it on through this system to the coming generations. The general secondary schools supply the reserves to the leading strata and the intelligentsia, and to a certain extent (as a by-product) to the lower and medium administrative levels as well. The specialised secondary and vocational training schools are intended to serve the reproduction of the skilled worker layer in the broadest sense of the term; the most successful students become lower and medium level technicians. Finally, those

114

who do not continue their studies beyond the primary school make up the majority of the unskilled and semi-skilled workers who in our society have the lowest level of prestige.

The training of skilled workers

From the point of view of our study, it is the system for training skilled workers which is of particular importance. Today it is perhaps precisely this stratum which is the most strongly bound by the ties of the division of labour, in comparison either with those in higher education or with unskilled workers. In order to be able to analyse this problem more closely, it is first of all necessary to outline briefly the major trends in this field which arise from the effects of technical progress. This is all the more important since hasty generalisations often make it difficult to understand the process as a whole. Frequently only one of the many aspects of this multidirectional development process is emphasised and, on the basis of technocratic illusions, the expected positive consequences of technical progress are overestimated. If we analyse the present situation, we can observe the following trends.

(1) The most important change, in the sense that it affects the greatest number of workers, continues to be the replacement of manual labour by mechanisation. The beginning of this process goes back to the period when the textile and metalworking industries emerged, but mechanisation continues to be a highly topical subject in many fields (for example in agriculture, in warehousing and the docks, in underground and surface construction, etc.). In the course of development, manual labour is replaced not by skilled labour but, in most cases, by semi-skilled, and this does not require the training of skilled workers in the traditional sense.

(2) Simultaneously with the first process, the old traditional crafts continue to lose their craft character and take on the characteristics of semi-skilled work. Because of technological progress, many jobs are narrowed down and the activities required become a routine. Today we can scarcely find a traditional craft to which this process would not apply and where, precisely for this reason, the need for a radical reform in skilled

worker training would not emerge.

(3) Technical progress creates new jobs in comparatively large numbers (the majority of these are, irrespective of their official classification, again of a semi-skilled nature, for example operators of automatic or semi-automatic machines, punch-card operators, etc.), but it only creates a small number of new crafts (e.g. television assemblers, or maintenance personnel for automated machines). The latter crafts are to some extent different from the traditional ones, first of all because in most cases they require less manual dexterity but a much greater general and specialised technical knowledge.

The technical basis for just about all crafts and jobs is continually changing. This change is often far-reaching, making the know-how which was previously essential obsolete and superfluous in a short space of time. Apart from the equalisation process which we have already mentioned, this fact in itself would justify the view which challenges the maintenance of the categories of skilled, semi-skilled and unskilled worker, and by the same token would suggest the elaboration of a new training system. In Hungary, the number of skilled worker trainees increased almost fourfold between 1953 and 1965. This can hardly be justified by the requirements of technical progress, since in Sweden this rise (from 1958) was only 27.6 per cent, in Austria 44 per cent and in Italy 46.5 per cent. It can be explained much more rationally by the fact that this form of training led to an apparent drop in the number of students failing to continue their studies after primary school, and helped to educate the young people to work. On the other hand, it served to protect children from being disillusioned, by moderating the aspirations which could be met at the present level of the division of labour, and by guiding them into suitable schools. The most detrimental effects of this phenomenon can mainly be found among young people who are in disadvantaged positions to begin with. The present system of skilled worker training can therefore be justly criticised, both from the point of view of efficiency (it is not suited to the changed requirements of technical progress) and from the point of view of socialist values (it turns people into the slaves of a craft or job for their whole lifetime).

116

Present contradictions

One of the obvious contradictions of our skilled worker training system is that although technical progress demands that the specific occupations entail knowledge which can be acquired within a short time by someone with a comparatively high general cultural level, many occupations of a semi-skilled nature have been categorised as skilled work because of wages policies and other reasons (particularly in light industry, commerce and the food trades), in spite of the fact that the requirements in these occupations have not changed. (Or if they have, it has been rather in the direction of restricting the knowledge and skills required.) While on the face of it this process serves highly positive goals — such as, among other things, raising the prestige of the occupations or crafts concerned — it has in fact rarely achieved this effect (one only has to think, for example, about whether a skilled character has actually been added to women's occupations in the textile industry). In general, it reduces the value of skilled labour even in occupations which really do require specialised knowledge. And from our point of view, it is not an unimportant point that a skilled worker's certificate, gained through some degree of effort, increasingly ties people to one detailed area of the job.

There has been a clear trend towards calling any form of semi-skilled work where there are shortages a "skilled trade". Furthermore, in those areas where the number of applications for the skilled workers' training schools is insufficient, a so-called "raised level" of education is introduced. For instance, training for sales personnel in the food trades takes place at the "raised" level, despite the fact that given a suitable level of general education, the knowledge needed to meet the demands of the job can be learned in a comparatively short time, and the emphasis should rather be placed on supplying continuous information to the sales personnel (on the properties of new commodities, on how to use them, on new commercial methods, etc.). One by-product of this process is the contradiction between the "unskilled" workers who are experienced in their jobs and those who, while having certificates of skilled training, have less experience. For in the majority of the trades and

117

jobs mentioned, practice, linked with certain personal abilities, is often worth more than the knowledge acquired in the course of vocational training.

The trends of technical development which we have outlined above result in the fact that, although there is a comparatively large amount of time available in the skilled worker training schools to learn the trade and acquire abilities, the education is not effective enough, for it is incapable of following practice. The problem is not alleviated if, in training, priority is given to educating skilled workers on a broader basis rather than with restricted specialisations, although this is clearly a positive endeavour. (In the past decade just about every country, including Hungary, has substantially reduced the number of trades taught.) This means that in the training of skilled workers, the emphasis is transferred from the acquisition of specific skills to more general technical knowledge; but for the most part this fails to secure a suitable standard of education in either respect, and students frequently resist theoretical subjects because they have different expectations from this type of school. Thus the goal of convertibility can only operate within narrow limits. The skilled worker training schools, particularly those which provide a certificate of completed secondary studies, have a tremendous task in raising the general cultural level of their students. This would serve to prevent their career opportunities being narrowed down, but in practice such a deep gulf exists between the general secondary schools and the vocational secondary schools that the right of students in the latter to continue their studies at universities and other institutes of higher education is rather theoretical, and this possibility in practice remains open only for people with exceptional talent. It is also worth noting that according to a study completed by the Ministry of Labour in 1970, only 12.3 per cent of students in vocational secondary schools originally wanted to learn a skilled trade.

It must also be remembered that our society not only requires the young person to choose an occupation at an age when his or her autonomy is in most cases a complete illusion, but it also makes an ideal of having a lifetime confidence in the trade thus "chosen", provides incentives for it, and not

118

infrequently even forces people into such behaviour, describing non-conformist conduct as an undesirable deviation. This is connected with and backed up by a type of planning which examines the expected numbers of workers in the various trades and even in precisely definable jobs, and works out definite recruitment plans accordingly. From this point of view "dropping out", like leaving an occupation, is considered a negative phenomenon which must be fought against, using administrative as well as psycho-technical and socio-technical methods. However, in some trades dropping out is taking place on such a broad scale that the deviational nature of the phenomenon itself becomes questionable. For instance, according to the Ministry of Labour survey already mentioned, there is a drop-out rate of 42.4 per cent among students in the agricultural trades. About one third of those trained take jobs outside their trades, as the relevant literature emphasises to the point of boredom. In addition, the rate of job changes among young skilled workers is quite high too, and since it often involves the abandonment of the trade learned, many regard it on the above grounds as a phenomenon to be condemned and to be prevented by administrative measures.

The facts which we have referred to are well-known, and they make it quite obvious that there is a crisis in vocational training. However, the recognition of this fact may lead, and indeed has already partly led, to many different proposals for solving it. Despite the variety of proposals made to date, we can distinguish two main tendencies, which differ on the basis of their view of the relationship between school training and the specific division of labour.

A new school model

Those who concentrate on school training are basically correct in their judgement of the weakest points in the present school system (these are noted in the new educational reform which is now under way), and their proposals contain a number of points worth considering. Nevertheless, they cannot change the present situation, since they do not touch upon its essence, on precisely those features which tie people to specific jobs

119

for a lifetime.

We, in contrast, feel that it is possible to develop a joint system of organising both production and school training, which does not fix a person's place in the division of labour for a lifetime but allows him to orientate himself continually towards finding himself and his identity, creating the possibilities and even the incentives for the worker to change his occupation or trade at any stage of his life. But in order to achieve this, the mechanical relationship between the current general system of school training and the world of work must first be broken.

The primary task of a school system providing general education is to educate man as a human being, and not as a worker who will have to fit into the division of labour, in other words, its task is to prepare people *to control their own social relations* and *to consciously shape their own destinies*. According to this model, general knowledge, in quantities which can be provided to everyone within the economic possibilities of the moment and in the context of the chosen values, should be given in a uniform type of school which not only declares but actually implements a final end to segregation. The system of vocational training, in its various levels and forms, should be sharply distinguished from this. In contrast to the former, the latter must genuinely provide the knowledge and abilities necessary for participating in some specific branch of the division of labour. According to this concept, special schools would be linked to the primary schools and made available to everyone. Some of these would provide certain *basic* vocational knowledge and abilities on various levels, while other schools of this type would qualify for *certain trades* or *certain jobs*. These special schools should be made accessible to everyone who has the general or basic vocational knowledge to enable them to complete their studies. This open nature of the scheme means more than the mere provision of legal possibilities: it also involves the necessity of overcoming, in the practical sense, the social barriers which currently face people in worse off positions.

No matter how important we consider the possibility of an equal start and the openness of society in general, without

120

deep-seated changes all this will remain at the level of liberal illusions. Without structural changes, the main lines of the existing structure of society will be reproduced, and in the final analysis will be preserved. The most important part of these structural changes is the creation of social domination over administrative power. However, the realisation of this goal requires a substantially higher general level of education, and many would consider even the present level of education as too ambitious. It would be difficult to deny that workers who have completed secondary studies generally expect more from their work, and the majority of manual occupations are not capable of meeting these expectations. But society may benefit more from this than it loses, because it may result in various dynamic changes within the organisation of labour.

The aim: to overeducate

The natural concomitant of the system we are proposing is to overeducate, in a dual sense. On the one hand, under this kind of training system the majority of workers will have attained higher levels of general education than the level which they directly need in order to perform the kind of detail labour which they are likely to undertake. On the other hand, there will be more workers with a vocational training that enables them to fill a given occupation than is actually needed. The fear of overtraining in this sense acts as a block to social thinking, and is one of the main barriers to the establishment of a way of organising production that approaches socialist values. What we have in mind is a modern form of organisation of labour which, assuming a given technological level, offers the individual worker greater autonomy, responsibility and decision-making capacity: the worker would not receive his task in the form of an order but, instead, would be responsible for a definite function. Better educated workers with greater demands could urge the introduction of technological changes, including those which are not simply, or not primarily, important from the economic point of view. One even more important fact about this is that with relatively more workers at a higher cultural level, and with the raising

121

of the general standard of work, a new stratum of workers will be developing. It will be capable of demanding and carrying out real social control over the administrative apparatus. At the same time, the members of this stratum will have greater opportunity for mobility as individuals.

There can no longer be any objection in principle to over-training people by giving them a higher level of general education. Those reservations which are raised are based generally on practical arguments. First of all they feed on the fear that the aspirations awakened by a higher cultural level and then left unsatisfied will operate as a source of discontent. Secondly, there are economic considerations, according to which any educational input which cannot be used directly in social production is inexpedient. The situation is different when it is a question of the other form of overtraining, that is, if more people learn a particular trade than is required at a particular moment. The first two misgivings, those about discontent and economic wastage, are complemented in this case by two political or ideological arguments which would appear to be quite important: fear of structural unemployment, and fear of the unplanned nature of the phenomenon. For this is indeed a negation of the system which tries to create harmony between the organisation of production and the formal schooling system by determining the precise ratio of various jobs and trades.

But if we assume a truly open society, then overtraining in the individual trades and occupations is an essential precondition for widening the scope of the individual person's autonomy in finding the place most suited to them within the existing division of labour; and more than this, it is also the necessary precondition for a dynamic structural change, and for ensuring that the people in the various jobs are the most suitable ones for performing those particular tasks. In other words, this is the only way to create a situation where the individual can actually choose from among many trades, occupations and jobs while at the same time the organisation also has the opportunity of choosing from among many applicants. This latter fact in itself will already increase the intensity of labour within official working time. All this would also help,

122

in the final analysis, to create a situation where the greater part of the time not spent at work could become genuine free time, and could eliminate the situation which we outlined in the first part of this essay. At the moment, for his low wages the worker currently performs his work at a low rate of intensity within his official working hours, and increases his income with wages procured outside official working time. The form of overtraining which we have referred to would, on the other hand, provide the incentive for people to choose trades or jobs more independently, and to make more sensible use of their free time for self-development and self-fulfilment.

In our opinion, it is precisely here that a sound connection can be established between the problem of free time and the suggested (and overdue) changes in the organisation of production, as well as between the vocational system of education and the general one; people will thus be able to move more freely in both spheres of their life, to increase their own autonomy and to realise themselves as human beings.

NOTES
1. J. Danecki, *Jednosc podzielonego czasu* ("The Unity of Divided Time"), Warsaw 1970.
2. F. Zweig, *The Worker in Affluent Society*, London, p. 253.
3. In Danecki, *op. cit.*, p. 272.

8
Maria Markus and Andras Hegedus

TENDENCIES IN MARXIST SOCIOLOGY IN THE SOCIALIST COUNTRIES

Ever since its inception, marxism has constantly raised and attempted to resolve a series of problems the scientific analysis of which is now considered as constituting the object of sociology. At the end of the last century this gave rise to an interpretation which tended to present the discussions going on within marxism as a confusion of ethics and sociology. This perspective was based on the argument that sociology ought to pursue the study of "natural scientific" truth, excluding all value judgements at the level of ethics.

Behind this very debatable interpretation there took shape an attempt to construct, on the basis of Marx, a sociology which would eliminate from marxism the value judgements pertaining to revolutionary commitment and raise it to the rank of science. This conception quickly revealed itself to be a deviation towards revisionism or purely rhetorical socialism.

Meanwhile, historical materialism continued to exist and to exercise its influence as an open theory attempting to preserve the unity of scientific vision and the critical and revolutionary attitude towards values. This is not only permitted but actually implied further development. A new and complex situation arose for marxist theory during the decades following the victory of the October revolution, a long period of transformation in official ideology marked by the reinforcement of tendencies towards simplification and vulgarisation. The free and lively discussions of the early period gradually disappeared; theoretical positions, transformed into official ideology, were complemented by dogmatic and apologetic positions. In the 1930s, this process gave birth to "histmat" as the general sociology of the Stalin period. It constantly proclaimed its scientific character, but in reality it rejected science to the extent that it refused to confront theory with social reality and did not recognise the necessity for social theory to develop any further.

The social changes which have occurred in the European socialist countries from the mid-1950s onwards (we cannot analyse them in detail here) are closely connected with the process of the rebirth of marxism. This process can be characterised as a "double movement", to use Lukács' expression: in terms of methodology, a return to Marx; in terms of problematic, the attempt to give a marxist explanation of contemporary social reality. (By the term "histmat" we mean not the basic principles of Marx's history of theory and society, but its vulgarised and distorted version, which emerged and became dominant in the 1930s and still holds its place in the economic text-books.) This return to reality on the one hand and to the marxist sociological tradition on the other has naturally resuscitated sociology as a specific social science.

Although this process was a turning-point in itself, it developed organically on the basis of the conditions prevailing at the time. Sociology was therefore used to verify and criticise the positions of "histmat" relative to socialism, positions which had been formulated in the 1930s.

However, there are two tendencies within this critical current. On the one hand, there is the tendency which is opposed to the axiomatic theses of "histmat" (often deriving from political considerations) and which seeks to emancipate sociology from any ethical orientation, to give it a scientific character. It denies any essential difference between the natural sciences and social science. On the other hand, a tendency is appearing which favours the development of a marxist theory of society. This tendency emphasises that it is necessary to construct theoretical positions with the help of analyses made on the basis of the marxist value-system and constantly confronted with social reality. These positions would be able to give an answer to the new problems posed by the development of society.

These main tendencies which we have described briefly are not yet clearly formulated and defined, and do not present themselves as schools with an elaborated system of concepts

125

and theoretical positions. The tendencies at present diverge mainly over the question of defining the role and social positions of sociology. This period could just as well have seen these differing approaches fusing as becoming increasingly differentiated. Nevertheless, the social conditions existing concretely in the socialist countries of Europe in our view tend to accentuate this divergence and not the opposite.

In these countries a relatively broad, although not homogeneous stratum has formed, the members of which, in the name of various individual interests, real or imagined, and even in the name of what are called "common interests", consider the most important goal of the social sciences to be the defence of the theoretical positions and institutions already established and the prevailing forms of control and management. They demand of marxist sociologists a party spirit in the strict sense of the term, and expect them to fulfil primarily an apologetic function. The origin of this attitude is without doubt linked to the fact that during the initial stage of socialism the victorious new social conditions had to be defended in a difficult historical context. In the USSR of the 1930s the "standard" arsenal of "histmat" fulfilled this "defensive" function with a certain degree of success. Today, in its ossified form, it is no longer capable of fulfilling this objective. Hence the various attempts to improve and "modernise" it.

As a rule, the traditional histmat "material" is modernised. First it is filled out with sociological ideas which do not appear to threaten its fundamental conceptions or the realisation of the objective it has set itself; then empirical sociological investigations are added which essentially serve more to illustrate the theoretical positions already taken than to confront these positions with reality and verify them experimentally. Thus the contribution of sociology serves mainly to demonstrate the progress made in the socialist countries through the use of statistics. This point of view is typically formulated in one of Academician Feodoseyev's articles: "The achievements of the Soviet socialist system must be demonstrated by sociological studies dealing with concrete reality."

It is on the whole characteristic of this tendency always to compare the results obtained by socialist society with

126

those of the capitalist past. Consequently, any historical change seems to be the direct result of socialist development; in most cases any real confrontation of the given situation with global historical reality is omitted.

One of the most important themes is to demonstrate how the cultural level of society or each of its strata has been raised, and their access to cultural values increased; this proves the superiority of the socialist régime better than the level of economic development does.

Basing themselves on Marx's tenet that men must be judged by their acts and not by their words (a thesis which is true in general but is extended here in too absolute a fashion), the representatives of histmat did not at first adopt so-called subjective methods in collecting sociological information. The attitude of men towards their work was measured solely by the achievement of norms and other economic indicators. This naturally led to a completely false conclusion: firstly, because economic indicators must be used with a critical mind as a result of the frequent divergences between statistical data and social facts (for example, a high attainment of norms may indicate not only intensive labour but also the lowering of the norm); secondly, because the actions resulting in these findings (e.g. the realisation of norms) may be caused by different motivations — the desire to make money by any means, a sense of the usefulness of work to society, identification with the work, etc.

This tendency could not of course avoid attempting to explain the causes of the various negative phenomena appearing in socialism (various aspects of crime, breaches of work discipline, the resistance of religious ideology, etc.). Yet this explanation is again based not on an analysis of social conditions but on a generalised supposition that consciousness will lag behind reality, that is to say that "relics" of capitalism survive in a socialist régime, in the value-system and the norms of human conduct. Hence the fashion for studying consciousness; despite great initial hostility, so-called subjective methods developed. But in spite of being more "sociologised", histmat showed itself incapable of satisfying the growing need for knowledge of concrete social reality. As we have already men-

127

tioned, this need first appeared largely at the level of theory, as the necessity for a confrontation between theoretical positions relative to socialism (which often declared that the social ideal had already been attained) and reality.

When the tendency towards rationalising the organisation of institutions and methods of control eventually developed almost throughout the socialist countries, a greater need for recourse to sociology and the socio-technical assistance it could provide was felt. This led sociologists not only to undertake intensive empirical studies, but also to support the tendency which refused *a priori* to concern itself with values. According to this tendency the purpose of sociology was solely to make specialised empirical studies with no value orientation. Consequently, by the term "empiricism" we refer not to the empirical study of society, but to this tendency, which conceives sociology solely as an a-theoretical science for which the scientific criteria of objectivity, rationality and precision represent the sole values. The attitude of histmat towards sociological empiricism thus conceived is highly equivocal. After an initial period of out-and-out hostility there came a phase in which it was more or less tolerated. This is not surprising, for if histmat is to acknowledge the existence of an independent sociology, empiricism, which excludes the notion of value from its orientation, is the most convenient formula. Its general perspective on determinism, which strictly limits man's freedom to act, is fairly easily reconciled with this empiricist tendency which conceives the whole of sociology on the model of the natural sciences. And to the extent that the empiricist tendency of sociology does not consider the choice and surveillance of values to be its task, it can in fact render great services to histmat in its defence of the social status quo, that is to say not only the development of socialism but also its prevailing form.

Not only histmat sociology, but also various other social sciences encourage an empiricism devoid of any ideology, for the upholders of the latter often demand that sociological activity be restricted to areas of empirical research which are still virgin territory. They thus prevent sociology from penetrating into other disciplines and tackling them with a critical

128

spirit. They basically ascribe to it an entirely auxiliary function — that of providing them with "raw material".

A phenomenon very interesting from the point of view of sociology is to be observed latterly within this tendency, especially in the USSR and in Poland. Numerous representatives of sociology "not orientated towards values" are abandoning concrete sociological research, which in any case is often not concerned with important social problems (on the whole limiting itself to description and short-term diagnosis). They concentrate their interest on problems of an entirely methodological character. This change is partly due to the illusion that the methodology of marxist sociology can be elaborated independently of the concrete study of important social problems. This partly means that they are refusing to confront these problems. or at least that they think they can be resolved by carefully perfected technical procedures. However, the empirical tendency by no means signifies that histmat has ceased to exist; situating itself in an entirely different perspective, it has not challenged its own theoretical foundations.

Nevertheless, the path of socialist progress is being taken in the socialist countries of Europe, and it is appearing as the inevitable expression of the contradictions of a centralised society and as a reaction against apologetics on behalf of established institutions. Basing itself on the values of marxism, this commitment demands genuine analysis of the prevailing relations so that positive paths for future development can be chosen on this foundation. In our country, the appearance of this current in particular enables critical analysis of the centralised economic system based on the plan to be undertaken; proceeding from this, a new model can be elaborated. Nevertheless, none of the sociological tendencies mentioned above corresponds to an orientation of this kind. Histmat sociology by its very nature allows institutions, theoretical positions and obsolete methods of management to be defended; it thus holds back progress. As for the empiricist tendency, it at best facilitates criticism of existing relations and institutions and the pursuit of optimum efficiency. It is precisely for this reason that a tendency has necessarily appeared in sociology which, while not denying the importance of theory, at

129

the same time recognises the necessity for empirical studies. For this tendency, theory does not constitute an "ideology" of existing reality but a means of formulating hypotheses of possible lines of development, and of indicating the possible choices between various social goals and the essential relations which the latter imply. It does not consider empirical study to be solely a social technique, but a scientific method which enables existing conditions to be analysed in real terms on the basis of the system of values we choose.

An approach of this kind is, in our view, the best one, and forms the basis for the development of marxist sociology. However, this tendency is not yet a developed theory. It is distinguished from the preceding tendencies more by its particular conception of the social role of sociology than by an elaboration into a homogeneous theoretical system. Today we can encounter this conception of marxist sociology in different countries, but if the efforts born of this conception are examined, it becomes apparent that they are largely connected with the different tendencies existing within marxist philosophy, which set out from very different theoretical principles. Thus for certain Yugoslav marxist sociologists, for example, a similar conception of the social role of sociology goes with an ethical interpretation of marxism. Among certain Soviet and Polish sociologists, it is linked to the utilisation of elements of structuralism or functionalism, etc.

As far as the authors of this essay are concerned, this approach is intimately bound up with the "socio-ontological" tendency in marxist philosophy, which rests on the same social forces. But whereas the main function of philosophy is to determine and justify the values chosen, the task of sociology is to undertake sociological analysis of different concrete solutions on this basis and to foresee the social consequences of the different variations.

Thus, the third tendency to be found in marxist sociology sets out from the thesis that at each given stage of history there are several possibilities for subsequent development. Whether or not they are conscious of it, the choice of this or that option for development depends on people. Consequently, sociology cannot be solely an "objective" science predicting the future exactly, for the positions one adopts in any description and forecast constitute a factor in the process of development. This does not mean that this value-orientated type of sociology has less objectivity or less scientific value than that based on a purely empirical approach to problems: it defines itself in the first instance by critical analysis of existing institutions, the processes occurring within society and the possible courses of future development undertaken on the basis of a consciously chosen course — in this case, the perspective of socialism. In other words, considerations not only of optimisation but also of the humanisation of social relations are involved. Consequently, sociology of this kind seeks primarily to achieve two objectives. First of all, it attempts to draw up a model of society realistic enough to endow men with a wider possibility of choice between the available alternatives; by this very fact it contributes to the real humanisation of social relations. Secondly, it compares existing institutions and social relations with the chosen hypothesis of development. It attempts to study them in their movement, in their contradictions, in their transformations, in the context of the consciously chosen perspective. This tendency does not contest the validity and practical utility of socio-technical research and methods; it does not demand that they support the alternative chosen when applied, or that they facilitate the realisation of the latter rather than having a contrary effect.

As we have tried to show above, the various tendencies have their own definitions of what the object and function of sociology within society consist of. Their centre of interest varies to a greater or lesser extent, according to the potential for social development and the pace at which it can proceed. Given that each of these tendencies studies the same social reality, they are certainly at variance with each other; each tendency must reply to the questions posed by the other (even if the questions are entirely "external" from its own point of view), for these often directly or indirectly challenge its own theses and methods, at times even the entire system of thought. A brief examination of certain debates which have taken place in recent years will enable us to demonstrate more concretely the originality of the methods of the tendencies described.

131

These debates cannot be understood if they are taken to manifest a divergence of views at the level of individuals. In order to analyse them intelligibly, not only the system of thought on which these tendencies are based, but also the social role they have assigned to themselves must be grasped. The debates which have arisen over the problem of alienation demonstrate this very clearly. They began as philosophical debates, but then they acquired a place of their own in marxist sociology, essentially because one's answer to them largely determines the conception one has of the social role of the sociologist. Although it is demonstrably one of the chief categories of Marx's historical and social theory, the very concept of alienation totally disappeared in the subsequent development of marxism, particularly in histmat theory. It is only with the general renaissance of marxism that it is again finding recognition; analysis of the reasons for this process would, however, go beyond the framework of this article.

The histmat view is based on the thesis that after a short transition period the socialist revolution brings about a society which, while of course it is capable of developing and improving, nevertheless basically possesses all the essential characteristics of socialism. Consequently, there is no place in this system for notions such as alienation or humanisation, for society is already considered humanised. However, to the extent that this tendency has been obliged to confront reality in the course of the debate, and to the extent that it uses the term alienation to designate unarguable "defects", the term at most refers to "relics" of capitalist society. These latter cannot find propitious soil in socialist society and still less can they give rise to forms of alienation.

"As a socio-economic system, there is no alienation within socialism," says L. Veresh, for example. "Non-antagonistic contradictions exist within socialism. They have their origin in the unequal levels of economic systems or in development which is insufficient by comparison with the higher stage of communism, in practical mistakes in economics and politics, and also in the influence of residual petty-bourgeois thinking."

Even though this quotation may appear a somewhat extreme definition and those taking this position often express themselves more subtly or make significant concessions, it is nevertheless a statement conforming to their view that socialist society has abolished private property and simultaneously abolished alienation as a structural phenomenon.

This view has a direct and considerable influence on sociological research, for it inevitably directs the sociologist towards the study of social problems in the superficial realm of phenomena rather than a search for their structured cause. Consequently, this tendency attempts to find a means of removing negative phenomena from the framework of given institutional options. As a sociological technique, an approach of this kind can explain social conflicts to a certain extent, but it does not facilitate the liquidation of outdated forms nor their replacement by new ones. On the contrary, it helps to maintain them.

The problem is posed very differently by the third tendency which we have attempted to define. It sets out from the idea that in doing away with private property the socialist revolution opens a new path for the development of society, but this does no more than furnish the possibility and necessary condition for new forms of social relations to be able to develop in every sector of life. The constant transformation of society, however, is necessary if this objective is to be attained, and in many respects such changes will be of an essential, qualitative nature. In order for the society born of the socialist revolution to be genuinely able to sustain the developmental dynamic that alone guarantees the realisation of the social conditions which it has set as its goal, it is equally necessary for it to be capable of continual critical analyses even in respect of its own newly created institutions. Consequently, the analysis of the problems of alienation and humanisation within socialist society directs the choice of hypotheses towards the most recent development in the view of this tendency. It thus facilitates social practice and enables society to measure the extent to which it has achieved these objectives, and to assess the objectives it must set itself for the future.

It is entirely evident that if one sets out from this conception no "dysfunctional" phenomenon arising in socialist society can be considered the result of subjective or even objective errors unconnected with the system, or as accidental defects. On the contrary, one necessarily arrives at a conception of their structural causes and goes on to recognise the fact that specific new forms of alienation appear in the course of the development of socialism. This, however, in no way means that there is any identity of views between this tendency and the one we have not specifically discussed, the tendency which analyses alienation solely in relation to the individual, using it only as a psychological concept to explain any conflict situation and thus transforming the concept of alienation into a magic and extrahistorical formula which cannot help in the understanding of social reality.

For the concepts of alienation and humanisation to serve as a theoretical guideline in the study of concrete relations and conditions, it is necessary to study the reality and model of the corresponding social structure. It is no accident that, next to the concept of alienation, there has been no problem more discussed in the marxist sociology that has developed over the last ten years than that of analysing the new structure of socialist society, the changes in it and the theoretical questions relating to these. The chief subject of discussion has been problems such as the following. Do social classes continue to exist in socialist society? In what proportion do different groups participate in the distribution of material goods, prestige and power? How far can the structure of socialist society be considered open or closed?

The histmat tendency considers the distinction between state and co-operative property to be an essential structural factor. Janos Blashkovich, for example, one of the representatives of this tendency, writes in his book on the problem of the concept of the working class: "To the question as to whether the significance of property relations has diminished within socialism, the reply must be unequivocally 'no'." It is true that two lines farther on, he comments: "Although one of the reasons for explaining the difference between the working class and the peasantry is the dual form of socialist property, these two classes are identical in terms of their relations with property." However, it is on the basis of the difference between state and co-operative property that two

134

essential classes are to be distinguished in socialist society, the working class and the peasant class; if the existence of other structural indications such as the difference between town and country, between manual and intellectual work are to be considered at all, these factors are considered secondary or dependent by comparison with the above-mentioned distinction.

One of the greatest problems of this tendency is to define the concept of working class, about which discussion has already been going on for some time on an international scale. The main question which poses itself is that of the integration of technical, economic and management cadres into the working class. In the socialist view, this thesis of integration is considered acceptable because a cadre from this stratum (a) already essentially stems from the working class; (b) has the same share in state property as the worker; (c) is indistinguishable in terms of income from a good skilled worker; his management activity is not in opposition to the worker because the cadre is not the representative of the capitalist proprietor. He occupies his managerial post in production solely because of the technical division of labour.

On this basis the view is taken that the entire management of the enterprise forms part of the working class, that is to say that it has no interests or goals different from the workers who perform physical work in the proper sense. Many representatives of this tendency count as part of the working class, men from the working class who have risen in the hierarchy, including those who have reached the highest seats of power. Another basic tenet, held by those who emphasise the essential role of property relations in the determination of the structures of socialist society, is the statement that the workers in the agricultural co-operatives form an independent "general peasant class", within which the "agrarian intelligentsia" is similarly integrated. This conception stems from the fact that a peasantry divided by the régime of private property is transformed after the socialist reorganisation of agriculture into a single class of co-operative workers, but it leaves aside the differentiation which has occurred among the members of the co-operatives through their different functions. It

135

clearly follows from this that by "enlarging" the working class and the peasant class, this conception does away with "the intelligentsia" and, at its most extreme, considers that section of the latter which is directly involved in material production to belong essentially to the working and peasant classes.

This view is formulated as follows in the discussion organised by the *Tarsadalmi Szemle* which we have already quoted: "Gradually the category of the intelligentsia will have to be abandoned, for, properly speaking, it is of little importance."

The most problematical aspect of this approach is the fact that it attempts to analyse the fundamentally different structure of socialist society in terms of class society. Although Lenin's definition of classes is not adhered to, a special concept of non-antagonistic classes is created for this purpose, although it is recognised that "these are by nature no longer classes".

This fidelity to concepts is chiefly explained by the fact that without them it would be impossible to defend this conception of power, about which we will go into in greater detail when we discuss the bureaucracy.

The second consequence of this approach is that the abolition of private ownership of the means of production appears not as the end but as the revolutionary beginning necessary for the conscious communist transformation of social conditions. In a given historical and social conjuncture this conception takes as its criterion the social differences existing between men and the position which they occupy in the labour process — which, despite the "egalitarian" ideology, inevitably leads to an unequal distribution of power, income and prestige.

This realisation opens up vast perspectives for sociological analysis and makes it possible to uncover conflicts which are familiar yet often directly or indirectly denied by the doctrine of social sciences, conflicts whose origin is in the structure, based on the division of labour. This structure gives rise within socialism to strata and groups of people who have individual interests and goals. Similarly, it is only on this basis that one can analyse such important problems as the degree of social mobility or the structural reasons for the absence of mobility, the problems of power and domination, and other problems of this kind.

From these two different conceptions of the structure of the socialist countries there flow two views, opposed to each other, concerning the essentials of the perspectives for future development. If one emphasises the significance of what distinguishes state from co-operative property, then in doing so one is assuming that if this difference did not exist, if in other words co-operative property were generalised at the level of "the whole people", the principal condition would be fulfilled for the birth of a qualitatively different society, communism. For the tendency which, in the creation of structures, attributes major importance to the position of people in the division of labour, the new, qualitative state of society will appear when this or that type of work no longer automatically determines the options one has for the development of one's personality and no longer limits personal autonomy.

The above shows that one of the most significant divergences between the tendencies currently existing in marxist thought relates to the conception of the structure of power in socialist society.

The view of histmat sociology on this question is based on the thesis (which in their opinion is beyond discussion) that every institution of the socialist state serves common interests, in so far as it is a workers' state under the control of the working class. The hegelian illusion repeats itself, but at a higher social level, in that it no longer refers to constitutional monarchy but to a socialist state which has abolished private ownership of the means of production. This assertion, however, is constantly belied not only by scientific observation, but by everyday experience.

The individual interests of the institutions of management, partly fostered by the state itself in order to increase their efficiency, manifest themselves in a number of undesirable forms, the most common of which are the claim that individual interests are those of the collectivity, the secret character of the questions which are fought out within the organs of management and which the public is not informed about, the defence of hierarchy even at the expense of rationalisation and efficiency, even if it brings with it conformity, attempts to monopolise professional know-how, refusal to make errors

137

of management public through self-criticism, etc.

Histmat sociology is of course able to study the structure of the organs of state and the causes of negative phenomena and conflicts, but in order to do so it has to add to its initial axiom a new thesis, which asserts that the appearance of negative phenomena in the structure of power is due to factors of a subjective nature, individual errors or objective conditions independent of the authorities, but in no case to the very principle of control and authority. This hypothesis, however, narrows the field of sociological investigation and relegates the sociological approach which seeks the structural determination of social phenomena to the background. At best, this limits research to a socio-psychological view of the problem.

Despite this narrow manner of tackling the study of the structure of power, socialist practice compels critical analysis and realisation of the fact that the different institutions of the socialist state do not only represent common interests, but indirectly and directly represent individual interests, which are generally presented as common to the whole of society. It is because of this that bureaucratic relations in the marxist sense of the term inevitably form in the management apparatus of socialist society. This, as we have shown, is due to structural phenomena and not to subjective errors. Recognition of this fact considerably widens the field of application of sociological analysis, permitting genuine study of the institutions of the state apparatus, which is considered as the locus where the interests of different social layers manifest themselves. Analysis can also be brought to bear on the very important question, for socialism, of how far the form of the established institutions enables the whole of society to regulate the power of those in authority, and how control over the different state apparatuses can be realised in relation to the whole society of direct producers.

We wish to emphasise once again that none of the tendencies we have examined here is homogeneous. Closer examination would permit divergences of view to be traced within each of them. It nevertheless seems to us very important to emphasise the opposition which exists between these tend-

138

encies, for an understanding of them is indispensable if the subsequent development of marxism is to be interpreted rationally. Without this it will be impossible to avoid unprincipled compromises and an eclecticism which cannot bring about a rebirth of marxist social theory. We have deliberately neglected tendencies which are clearly bourgeois here, tendencies which also exercise a certain amount of influence in the various socialist countries. Marxist sociology is obliged to combat them daily. This question alone would require an entire essay in itself.

9
Maria Markus and Andras Hegedus

THE ROLE OF VALUES IN THE LONG-RANGE PLANNING OF DISTRIBUTION AND CONSUMPTION

Economists and sociologists in European socialist countries are asking increasingly often whether the specific features of the consumption structure which has historically come into being in these societies will be maintained in the context of a rising standard of living, or whether perhaps a change to a model more appropriate to a higher level will have to occur. Will it be possible, in the latter case, to follow the path trodden by the economically developed western countries, or will it be necessary to find ways that are more appropriate to socialist aims?

This question is particularly topical in Hungary. The new economic reform, which chiefly affects the sphere of industrial production, brings with it the need for changes in other aspects of social life too. Their integration in a comprehensive programme of social transformation, of which a long-range model of distribution and consumption is an organic part, is an essential precondition for the success of the economic reform too. What follows is a sociological approach to a number of problems connected with this task.

Certain methodological problems connected with the long-range planning of distribution and consumption

There are two extremes which threaten the long-range planning of consumption and distribution, as they do every other kind of socio-economic planning in general:

(a) *Voluntarism,* or the neglect of the real situation, an

attitude which includes constant reference to social laws. It is often linked with the idea that social progress, like natural processes, is governed by laws that are essentially independent of the human will. According to this view, all that planning must do is discover these laws and help them to become effective. But in view of the fact that these laws can be formulated only in the most general terms, and that the formulation itself is arbitrary, this conception opens the door for a form of planning that takes no account of realities, and even itself serves as the ideological foundation for this kind of planning.

(b) As a reaction against the voluntaristic method of planning, a *"scientistic" planning* has taken shape in the socialist countries; this imagines itself to be free of ideology, and it relies on a wealth of empirical data without dealing with all questions in a pragmatic manner, without scientifically analysing the aims themselves. It maintains that establishing aims and objectives is the business of politics, and that the functions of planning are limited to elaborating the methods most suitable for realising these pre-established aims. We naturally do not deny that the determination of aims and objectives is, in the last resort, the function of politics. But this political activity must be submitted to control by public opinion and it must also be subjected to analysis by the social sciences, if we wish to avoid a situation where particular interests of certain narrow groups achieve a decisive role in this process.

It is only natural that this tendency should have led to the growth of a considerable mathematical apparatus, and that it has thus helped to raise planning to a more exact and scientific level than the one discussed earlier. Nevertheless, since it is not prepared to undertake either a conscious choice of values or, therefore, a scientific analysis of objectives, it also impoverishes planning.

These are, of course, extremes. In practice they rarely occur in such pure forms. It has, in fact, become noticeable lately that the first of the two methods of planning mentioned above has begun to make use of certain exact mathematical methods, without however changing in its essence.

We start from the general idea that in social reality there

141

exists a relatively wide range of possibilities of development, and so there is always room for conscious choice. The future, as far as we are concerned, is therefore not some sort of system or chain of necessary events which can be discovered in advance, but the result of human activity which, though limited in a certain way at every given *historical moment*, is not unequivocally determined.

For this very reason, the essence of long-range planning cannot be reduced to outlining in the form of hypotheses what changes are likely to occur in the long run in various fields of economics, or of social life in general; it has to elaborate those objectives which are part of a programme of social change in such a way that the appropriate analysis of empirical data is combined with the conscious choice of values. These objectives must reckon with realities and therefore be realisable. In this way the long-range plan (which includes the objectives of social change), the means needed to achieve them, and the prognoses which outline the expected consequences, form the basis for the elaboration of the social programme, including contingent variations.

Every social prognostic in its essence relies on two methods: extrapolation and interpolation. The first establishes past trends in the economic, cultural, etc. development of individual countries and projects them into the future. In other words, it means that a given society must use its past experiences when outlining its own future. The latter interpolation is based on trends discerned in countries that are in advance of the country doing the planning, in other words, on the use of the experiences of societies other than that whose future is predicted. Since prognostics based on both extrapolation and interpolation by their very nature remain within the framework of past historical experience, they cannot in themselves constitute the basis for a long-range plan aiming at the *transformation of the existing social conditions*.

Interpolations and extrapolations, as well as the prognostics relying on them, must be subjected to criticism on the basis of a chosen system of values, in order to establish the effective causes of the trends of development outlined, *and the direction and cost of the changes that would have to be made from a*

142

socialist point of view. It is only on the basis of such a critical analysis that programmes, i.e. concrete objectives and the means needed to realise them, can be elaborated.

The practice of planning thus leads to long-range programmes through a critical evaluation of prognostics. These programmes are then expressed in a temporal context in the form of concrete plans.

For well-known ideological reasons, extrapolation was given preference in the socialist countries as soon as voluntarist planning methods were recognised to be outdated. This was supported by the view, which continued to dominate, that in the socialist countries new social conditions had already been created that could develop further without necessitating additional *fundamental* social changes. According to this view, the only factor making for uncertainty in planning based on extrapolation was the fact that one could not reliably predict technological progress. It is usually on this basis that a distinction is made between phenomena which are unequivocally determined and those predicted only with a certain amount of probability. But this is only one of the factors which determine the limits of the use of extrapolation.

Even more important is the fact that what is extrapolated is always *an existing structure,* with existing proportions and tendencies, and the method of extrapolation does not take into account the possibility that these might be significantly changed by human action — action whose course is not predetermined by some sort of general laws, but is the result of conscious choices of values. All this of course does not mean that there are no technical interdependences which have to be borne in mind when choosing alternatives, nor that the limits of extrapolation cannot be significantly expanded by optimum programming in the interests of this or that chosen objective. It is also true that simulation models also help to reduce the deficiencies of the method of extrapolation, principally by permitting the elimination of various unrealities. The practice of planning in Hungary provides many concrete examples of these.

The mechanical application of methods of extrapolation is most likely to produce serious mistakes in areas which, for some historical reason, are characterised by structural deficiences or which are unduly underdeveloped in comparison with the general level of our socio-economic development. The housing situation may serve as an example: the rate at which housing is constructed in Hungary is below that in capitalist countries at a similar stage of development.

The past, too, provides many examples of the serious mistakes produced by an uncritical application of extrapolation. Thus because of the fast rate of growth natural to the period of post-war reconstruction, groundless long-term predictions concerning socialist economic development were made.

In recent years in socialist countries, those concerned have made more and more use of the methods of interpolation in addition to those of extrapolation. This derives from the conviction that there is a model of civilisation which applies to the development of backward countries. Presuming normal development, the argument runs, one can say that similar levels of economic development will produce in various countries ways of life and patterns of consumption that closely resemble each other, since, after all, needs and ways of life are largely determined by the standard of living which in turn depends on the level of the economy.

It is certainly true that developing countries — and the socialist countries are no exception in this respect — tend to take over the cultural pattern of consumption of the economically more advanced ones. In the socialist countries this effect partially depends on the degree of openness shown by the society, an openness which is made almost inevitable by the fast development of mass communications, and partially on the extent to which the socialist countries are able to produce their own model of consumption which, while including the true values and achievements of civilisation, at the same time does not adopt the distortions which manipulation has produced in Western patterns of consumption.

The claim that, according to experience, the first of the above-mentioned effects is continuously growing, constitutes the basis of such theories as the much-discussed theory of convergence. There are also strictly economic theories which point in the same direction. The application of the method of

144

interpolation has been greatly encouraged in the past few years by the theory of structural analogy and that of iso-morphism, elaborated by cybernetics and also used by the social sciences.

The result of all this is a peculiar situation. The method of interpolation is becoming more and more widely used in long-range planning in socialist countries, and this naturally has an effect on economic theory. At the same time, at the level of official ideology there still survive conceptions accord-ing to which the socialist and capitalist countries necessarily diverge in every respect. Those who hold this opinion are not prepared to accept the facts indicating that parallel phenomena appear in differing socio-economic systems which have achieved the same level of economic development.

The question as far as we are concerned is not whether there are facts which show the existence of such tendencies, but the extent to which we must accept these as necessary and unchangeable. There is no doubt that technological progress in itself produces a whole series of identical or similar prob-lems, but this by no means implies that they must in each case be solved in the same way. In our opinion it is possible to create a pattern of civilisation, in other words a way of life and structure of consumption, which is appropriate to socialist aims and objectives, and we must endeavour to bring it about. In other words we conceive divergence to be not something inevitable, but a programme, an objective.

Both methods of prognostics discussed above provide neces-sary data for planning, but the only question they answer is "what will happen if . . .?" The planners, on the other hand, have to establish objectives within the realm of possibility. The question they have to answer is "what should happen?" To be able to do this, a value system is needed which can guide choice in a determined direction.

That is why marxism always connects scientific prediction with the struggle of various social forces and movements for the realisation of their objectives envisaged on the basis of a chosen system of values. As Gramsci put it: "In reality one can predict scientifically only the struggle, but not its concrete moments. They can only be the result of clashes between

145

contradictory forces which are in continuous movement and which cannot be expressed quantitatively. . . . In reality we can 'foresee' only to the extent that we can make conscious efforts, and thus in practice contribute to the coming about of the 'foreseen' event."

As the past few years tellingly illustrate, the struggles of various social forces seriously influence the way social progress is shaped, and so predictions often turn out to be erroneous.

This marxist notion was pushed into the background in the vulgar-determinist planning practice criticised above. Today value-orientated thinking — "value" taken in the philosophical and not in the economic sense of the term — has an increasing role even in bourgeois economics and sociology.

One of the basic dilemmas of planning which is based on differences in the system of values is the frequent differentiation between objectives directed towards economic optimisation and those aimed at the humanisation of social life. In the initial period of socialism, because of backwardness and isolation, the emphasis was on the primary accumulation of capital and the development of heavy industry and this led to a state of affairs where the question of optimisation as well as that of humanisation were pushed into the background. After the ending of the period of postwar reconstruction, however, it became quite clear that the rate at which the socialist economy developed was not satisfactory. Extraordinarily sharp contradictions appeared between the real development of the economy and those politically determined objectives which declared that the productive level of developed countries had to be reached in an impossibly short time.

These objectives proved to be unrealistic. The most that can be done is to exceed the rate of growth of capitalist countries on a similar level of economic development, and to lessen the gap in relation to developed capitalist countries. This, however, on its own, without solving problems of a different kind, has certainly not been sufficient to prove the superiority of the socialist system unambiguously. It is no less important to establish the sort of social relations under which every member of society can, in accordance with the economic level reached, maximally develop his personality and

146

realise it in his everyday life, that is both in his work and in his leisure activity.

Many subordinate these tasks and objectives of humanisation to economic effectiveness, and mechanically identify the latter with a rise in the standard of living. The popularity of this point of view is supported by the ideological attitude which argues that socialism as such has already succeeded in establishing humanised social conditions, and if these sometimes do not appear effectively in the everyday life of society, one has to blame economic backwardness. The rate of economic development naturally imposes significant limitations on the solution of the problems of humanisation. At the same time, though, an identical economic level permits solutions of very different values as regards the human aspect of social relations.

In our opinion the right combination of the objectives of optimisation and those of humanisation forms a basic part of long-range planning. When we argued earlier that it is possible to develop a socialist pattern of civilisation, we meant that this offers more to people, not perhaps by a speedier growth in economic efficiency, but by establishing a new, more humanised type of social relationship. All this does not mean, of course, that we want to deny the necessity of increasing the rate of economic growth, which is unsatisfactory at present, so that it will at least exceed that of capitalist countries on a similar level of development.

The socialist cultural pattern must not of course be looked at as some sort of necessary road for further development, predetermined by unchangeable laws of society, but only as an alternative, the realisation of which is historically possible, but which can only come about as a result of the struggle of various social forces.

Tendencies towards social equality and social differentiation in the socialist countries

Since the structure of consumption largely depends on relations of distribution, one of the most important questions as regards the socialist model of consumption refers to the degree and nature of desirable or permissible differences between

147

various strata of society.

Differences in income are usually justified in part ideologically, by the well-known principle of distribution according to the labour supplied, and in part practically, as providing incentives for a higher performance. In practice, however, differences appear which cannot be properly justified by either one or the other of these points of view. This is particularly true of the "hierarchical" differentiation of incomes (i.e. according to the position in the social division of labour), which tends to increase in the European socialist countries.

It is well-known that the classics of marxist literature did not consider such differences to be justified. Moreover, they considered their very existence to constitute a danger of bureaucratic distortion of socialism. This was connected with their notion that socialism would produce direct democratic forms of self-government which would become dominant. This road, however, proved to be impractical. On the contrary, in every European socialist country without exception the separate apparatus of professional management has continually grown. To ensure its professionalism and effectiveness a higher-than-average income has to be allotted to those in positions of greater responsibility. Proportions, however, have in many cases become distorted as a result, on the one hand, of stressing the hierarchical differences too strongly, and, on the other, of the lack of connection between high incomes and real performance. These distortions, for example, became very apparent during the 1968 distribution of enterprise profit when, though we were barely beginning to introduce the new economic mechanism, the key of distribution made a considerable difference between the three pre-established groups of personnel, which could have been justified only if the risks and the responsibilities of the executives, and thus their effectiveness, had been proportionally increased. (We do not wish to imply that the new mechanism itself created these differences, only that on the one hand, it obviously strengthened them, and on the other, it brought them out into the open, which incidentally is in itself of positive importance.)

Differentiation according to hierarchical levels within socialist society does not appear merely in incomes. It has other

148

forms too, which are frequently disguised and therefore most difficult to control. In the first place this concerns the goods and benefits which are generally considered socially desirable, but which are in short supply. Their distribution sometimes takes place in a preferential way and they become part of the privileges of certain strata of society, and this leads to considerable injustices. For example, in the distribution of housing certain groups of executives and professionals have in the course of the past twenty years achieved a position of privilege, so that their members find it easier to obtain housing, in this way receiving allotments roughly equal to between five and ten years' wages of an average worker. This is especially worthy of attention, since early on — and not without foundation — the sort of illusion was born that it is precisely in this field that distribution in accordance with the principles of equality has become a fact. As certain sociological studies have shown, allocation by the authorities systematically favours the occupational groups of higher income. High-standard, low-rent state housing, requiring no prior payment, is allocated to the higher income groups in a considerably greater proportion than to the lower ones. The latter, in order to improve on their housing situation which is worse to start with, are generally forced to build or to buy an apartment. Significant differences between groups appear not only in their chances to have housing allocated to them, but also in respect of conditions on which they acquire housing when they do not get it free of charge.

According to this survey by Szelenyi and Konrad (1969), the various income groups spend on housing the following sums to complement their housing needs:

				in forints:
the upper group ...	...	...	...	51.000
the upper middle group ...	...	...	47,000
the middle group	...	...	...	69,000
the lower middle group ...	...	...	82,000
the lower group ...	...	...	...	73,000

"This tendency is so strong," the authors tell us, "that the readiness to bear material burdens in order to improve their housing situation shows a similar distribution in terms of occupational groups."

Though the upper income groups spend significantly less on housing, their housing situation is much better, and this applies to density as much as to equipment and location.

The distribution of housing is only the most characteristic of the hierarchical, non-wage differences in distribution, but it is a long way from being the only one. Everyone is well aware of the advantages which certain groups enjoy when it comes to buying or using cars, getting grants for holidays at resort places, buying building lots and so on, which are normally not taken into account when one reviews income differences.

It often seems that these privileges are offered in the interests of enterprises, or even because of wider social interests (for example, in using housing — allocation to facilitate the recruitment of suitable personnel) but in reality this applies only to a small proportion of the cases, and even then it would probably be better to express this openly, in the form of money grants. In that way public opinion would be in a better position to estimate the extent of existing differentiation.

While the differences *between* hierarchical levels have become exaggerated as if to compensate for this, on the *same* levels there has come into being an extreme equality, in spite of all the efforts of central authorities to counter this. There is *no proper differentiation according to performance,* though that is one of the basic preconditions of a more dynamic economic development.

Differentiation in accordance with performance can be applied not only to individuals, but also to enterprises, as is presupposed by the new economic mechanism. Workers will be paid more for the same work by more profitable enterprises. This is a precondition for effecting the necessary structural changes in industry and for utilising the labour force in a more effective way, which constitutes the mainspring of economic development.

Differentiation between enterprises will evolve if the various mechanisms of the new economic system are applied consistently. Differentiation according to performance within any individual enterprise will, on the other hand, come into being only if a significant process of democratisation takes place within the enterprise, that is, if the collectives of workers are given a real opportunity to control effectively the various levels of management. This is the only way to put an end to the legitimate fear of the workers (which is the main obstacle in the way of systematic application of differentiation according to performance) that the management will base the work evaluation not on their real performance, but on personal relations and considerations, so that this type of differentiation would mean a strengthening of their personal dependence.

It is clear from the above that we in no way doubt the need for differentiation up to a certain point. *What we consider unacceptable is the further growth of hierarchical differentiation,* that is, differentiation according to rank. On the contrary, we advocate measures which up to a point would produce a reverse effect. This appears all the more justified since the high incomes which arise as a result of this differentiation do not always lead to a higher level of consumption in the social groups concerned, sometimes because of the lack of corresponding needs, sometimes because of the insufficiency of the available goods. So we can note recurring signs of the involvement of these groups in types of speculative activity (building lots, houses, etc.). Necessary social differences must be kept strictly under control, and every endeavour must be made to ensure that they are not inherited, that the opportunities of the younger generation should be determined to as small as possible an extent by the place their parents occupy in the system of the division of labour, and by their better or worse position in regard to the distribution of goods.

Certain problems associated with the development of a socialist pattern of needs and consumption

In order to express our views on a socialist model of consumption we must differentiate between two types of personal consumption, basic and differentiated consumption, which do not involve a socialist society in identical obligations.

We mean by "basic consumption" a consumption minimum which varies with the cultural and economic level of develop-

ment and which must be assured by a socialist society for every member of it. The securing of this minimum for everyone must be a social objective even if certain strata or groups of society have not yet formulated the corresponding needs.

We speak about differentiated consumption in cases where the level of production and the forms of consumption permit — at least for certain individuals, groups or strata — a consumption higher than the basic level or a way of satisfaction of the basic needs differing from the standard one.

Both types of consumption are dynamic. They are basically determined by two factors, the economic level of the given society and the chosen system of values, and it is on the basis of the latter that we make a distinction between basic and differentiated consumption.

In the given circumstances of Hungary, at the present level of national income and dynamism of economic life, what can be considered basic consumption is food, clothing and housing necessary to ensure a healthy way of life, and a chance to educate oneself and one's family regardless of financial circumstances. As far as the latter is concerned, more than just a sort of minimum standard, applied to food, clothing and housing, must be considered part of basic consumption. It must include a free and limitless opportunity for education (within the range of possibilities offered by the society), regulated by the ambition and ability of the individual. It is of course not sufficient to have a system of values in order to establish concretely the standard and structure of basic consumption within a given society. A number of economic calculations must be made which collate objectives and opportunities.

Ensuring such a level of basic consumption for everybody must be considered — beside the continuous expansion of differentiated consumption — an indispensable feature of the socialist pattern of consumption.

Guaranteeing a basic level of consumption is particularly important from the point of view of the young. Socialist society has certain additional responsibilities in this respect. Not only the basic needs of the young must be ensured, but such conditions must also be created that would more and more equalise their opportunities for differentiated consumption too, so that their differentiated needs, and the possibility and way of satisfying them would not be determined purely by the social position of their parents. It is only the conscious and deliberate shaping of a socialist pattern of consumption that can counterbalance the effects of a structured society on the young, effects which specify different starting points and different life possibilities for the young members of different social groups.

Basic consumption cannot be ensured merely by making money available, since it is always possible to spend money, a general means of exchange, on satisfying needs which are not basic. This bears heavily on those (children, members of the family who are not earning etc.) who are not in a position to decide on the way money income is to be spent. It is precisely for this reason that the endeavours to reduce benefits in kind give cause for concern, as do also those which wish to tie them to the bread-winner, and practically to convert them into a kind of additional wage.

One cannot ensure an equal start for the young using only the means of monetary distribution, by raising family allowances, for instance. New types of benefits in kind must be created and the existing ones must be expanded. Thus the network of kindergartens and boarding schools must be thoroughly developed and school-books and certain cultural opportunities must be made available free of charge.

On this basis we can approach the question of general education too. In this respect socialist countries really ought to exceed the level reached by capitalist countries enjoying a similar national income. In order to ensure equal starting opportunities, the first thing that must be done is to equalise the educational level of the primary schools. The significant differences which still prevail in them further narrow the chance of obtaining higher education for children belonging to families that live in difficult financial and cultural circumstances. For this reason we must, on the one hand, extend the system of boarding-schools, and, on the other, apply deliberate preferences to schools that are handicapped, for instance, when modern teaching aids (television, audio-visual techniques, etc.) are distributed.

As to the raising of the school-leaving age, a project with

which we entirely agree in the long-run, we consider that at present making one or two years of nursery school more generally available is more important than increasing the number of years spent at primary school. (This proposal has, by the way, already been formulated in the long-range planning work of the National Planning Bureau). One reason for this is that the equalising effect of educational institutions is highest when the pupils are young, as has been shown by a considerable amount of research. Cultural differences that are established in childhood are difficult to overcome later.

It is often said that the raising of the level of general education increases social discontent, since it prompts people to make the sort of demands as regards both their type of work and their social position in general which at the given level of the social division of labour and of the national income cannot be satisfied. This is partially true, but this type of dissatisfaction can largely promote social changes — in the division of labour, in technology, and so on — which are in accord with the objectives of a socialist society. Raising the general level of education is advantageous from the view-point of the national economy too, since it makes it possible for individuals to adapt themselves more quickly to technological progress. (These days we often spend too much time, especially in the training of skilled workers, on making people learn obsolete knowledge, or knowledge that is fast becoming obsolete).

What is perhaps even more important is that a rise in the general cultural level promotes the process of making society more democratic, since it allows its members to comprehend relationships that are often very complex. In this case, then, education does not merely serve the upward mobility of individuals, as has generally happened in the past twenty years, but it ensures that those directly concerned with production and services can play their part in social control and this can partially compensate also for the sort of dissatisfaction which arises from ambitions not being satisfied in the immediate process of work because of its specialised character.

What also leads to dissatisfaction today is that people with a higher-than-average level of education (i.e. high-school graduates) are still in a minority in jobs with lower prestige, but this situation will be relieved as the general level of education rises.

Housing is, next to education, the other important component of basic consumption today. What is needed above all in this respect is a speeding up of the rate of building. In this respect, too, the requirement (far from being realised today) that we should build more dwellings than capitalist countries with the same national income per head of the population seems to be entirely justified. Only a significant increase in the number of dwellings can ensure adequate housing, satisfying the generally accepted social norms for every member of society, regardless of the position of his family. (This, of course, does not mean that every member of society must live in these standard conditions. Differentiated needs exist, and continuously grow in this field too, and society must also strive to meet them.) This is also connected with the already mentioned requirement of concentrating the resources of society in order to equalise as far as possible the conditions under which members of the new generation make their start. This demands radical changes, especially in housing. It follows from this that in case of dwellings satisfying only basic needs, the rent must not be raised from the present low level to one adequate to the market conditions. The highest they should go is to cover the costs of repair (which would also involve a certain rise). Market conditions should be relevant only to housing which satisfies differentiated needs. This means, of course, that the rent of state-owned housing satisfying such needs could, and should, be raised in this way. This principle must be applied also to the allocation of housing: dwellings satisfying the requirements of basic needs ought to be allocated free of charge. On the other hand, in the case of dwellings satisfying differentiated needs, the additional building costs ought to be borne by the new tenant, regardless of his social position. Those who build their own houses, privately or co-operatively (provided this is really for the satisfaction of their own housing needs) ought to be subsidised up to the standard cost level of state house-building, if they place their former dwelling at the disposal of the state.

Though this sort of system would lessen the unfounded advantages of some groups and individuals, they are still bound

155

to continue, until everybody is satisfactorily housed.

In our opinion one of the most important objectives of the long-range plan for the next twenty years must be the creation of a situation where a dwelling that at least satisfies the requirements of what we call basic consumption is available to everybody. This should be a right which the state guarantees to every member of society, one which should not be handicapped by high rents.

We therefore do not agree with the opinion which has become fairly widespread and which was most tellingly expressed by Tibor Tiska that "it is to the advantage of both the state and the population if people receive a higher income covering the rise in the rents, so that rents that express the market situation can be paid".

Compensation for higher rents in money "in proportion to the size and income of the family" does not solve the problems we have raised, since it virtually maintains, moreover it increases, the likelihood that the housing situation be further differentiated even below acceptable minimum standards.

Education and housing are not traditionally considered as basic needs as food and clothing. We emphasise them, nevertheless, since in our opinion they will be at the centre of attention in the next twenty years, and the resources of the national economy must be concentrated on them. This does not mean, of course, that we consider that food and clothing are no longer a problem for some groups of society, and that in this sense the problem of poverty has been solved.

The number of those in distress and, in a wider sense, of the poor, is relatively small today, but if we take no notice of them, or rather if we do not accept that the satisfaction of basic needs ought to receive preference in the plan, it may well increase. This problem also occurs in a special way in the gypsy problem. Their sub-culture involves them in a way of life which is not "civilised". We do not want to go into detail, but on working out the relevant plans one must bear in mind for the solution of the question not only that finances are required, but that the real results of a mechanically applied policy of assimilation ought to be re-examined.

It is necessary to continue subsidising basic foods in the interests of the fight against poverty — at least until one cannot ensure that everybody can satisfy his basic needs in the sense discussed above, even if prices are determind by market relations. The solution of this problem would be speeded up by expansion of school and kindergarten meals, and that of public catering at reasonable prices in civilised circumstances.

What we have emphasised in the above is the satisfaction of basic needs, which is only one of the aspects of the socialist consumption pattern, though in our opinion, at least under present circumstances, the most important one. In the long run, however, the expansion and appropriate satisfaction of differentiated needs will have an increasing importance.

In a dynamically developing society, once a certain level is reached, man is prompted to work first of all not by the necessity of satisfying basic needs, and hence not by the fear of hunger and poverty, but by the wish to satisfy his fast-growing differentiated needs. This makes it possible for a socialist society, once a certain level has been reached, to exclude the satisfaction of basic needs from the system of incentives, that is, to make them independent of the labour supplied.

And just because of this, it is more important to make possible the satisfaction of differentiated needs with appropriate goods and services, in order to give full effect to their function as incentives.

Differentiated consumption does not only promote economic development, it also allows the many sided development of the human personality. Naturally, not every differentiated need and its satisfaction has this effect. There is also what we call status consumption, i.e. consumption linked to one's status in society, a well-known phenomenon and serving first of all the satisfaction of manipulated needs.

One cannot, of course, divide up consumer goods and services in terms of whether they help to develop personality or merely satisfy the need for a certain status or prestige. Some of them are completely neutral in this respect, and what is even more important, the same object of consumption can fill different roles in different concrete situations.

One reason why we do not want to analyse this problem in detail in this paper is that the existing patterns of consumption

157

in today's Hungary are still first of all characterised by the fact that *real* needs are not sufficiently satisfied. Though in certain groups of society one can already notice phenomena associated with status and prestige consumption, this cannot as yet be clearly distinguished from the satisfaction of differentiated needs, since it is directed in the first place towards those objects and services, which are not yet generally available but for which a widespread demand already exists.

Our emphasising the requirement for differentiated consumption to mainly serve the development of the personality is not in opposition to the satisfaction of certain needs in a collective way. In the recent period, a tendency towards the growth of individualistic and commodity-centred attitudes has been discernible in several socialist countries, including Hungary. This, to a certain extent, is a reaction against the excessive collective attitude largely derived from poverty and characteristic of the first period of socialist development. The real problem appears when needs can be satisfied in both a collective and an individual way. In many cases the collectivistic solution is justified already by purely economic motives, but often its choice is supported also by other important considerations, for example, by the fact that in this way a certain service, or a type of commodity, becomes available to wider sections of society, and, what is more, may become a factor in the shaping of a new way of life.

Naturally this does not mean that we would advocate forcing a collective type of consumption on the population. What we argue is that we must create genuine alternatives concerning ways of life, too, and moreover, in such a way that the collectivistic solution should enjoy a certain economic preference. These days an opposite tendency can be noticed: in many cases there exists practically no possibility of choice any more, and needs can often be satisfied only in an individualistic manner. The maternity allowance is most instructive in this respect. It is a really serious help to those mothers who cannot find any way of taking care of their children, but on the other hand, if it is accompanied by a slowdown in the rate at which infants' nurseries are built, it will force mothers, with the exception of those whose earnings are really high, to interrupt their employment.

Similar problems appear in many fields of social life. Thus the expansion of trade-union and enterprise opportunities for holidays and relaxation has not kept up with the growth of the demand for them; and things like automatic laundries, common play or television rooms etc. are not yet borne in mind when planning new housing estates.

Pushing collectivistic solutions into the background directly promotes the diffusion of such specific features of the Western living pattern as the social seclusion of the families, the formation of an apolitical attitude, and of an exaggerated commitment to material goods.

The question may arise whether it is possible at all to influence the scope and character of the existing needs of a society. Another question would be, in what should we wish to achieve our consumption objectives without, for instance, limiting supply? Certainly, limiting further supply is likely to produce a considerable discontent in society.

The changing of needs is of course a continuous process of such a nature that it takes place even if conscious, deliberate influence does not play any significant role in it. The "social production" of needs is above all determined by factors such as technological progress, which creates new needs, or makes it possible for old ones to be satisfied in a different way; the growth in productivity of labour, which essentially determines the general level to which consumption can rise; the proportions and relations of distribution which concretely determine the level of consumption for various classes and groups within society, and through this, to a certain extent also its structure. The role of traditions, habits, norms, and value systems accepted by the society as a whole or by some groups in it, is also far from being insignificant. They determine to a greater or lesser extent the pattern of consumption which is considered socially desirable, and in this way they affect needs too.

It is also most important to bear in mind that those elements which truly become part of people's everyday activity prove to be most lasting in the structure of needs. Their character is also largely determined by the nature of this activity.

Besides the fact that decisions concerning the above-mentioned technical and economic factors indirectly affect the shaping of needs, the state has two other means at its disposal through which it can directly influence the formation of needs: the conscious and deliberate forming of the system of values (with the help of schools, adult education, and through the means of mass-communication), and direct advertising for certain goods. Though both are necessary, they do not have equal value for a socialist state. At the same time, because of the profit-orientation of industrial production, the second one (advertising) is receiving more emphasis, though it is essentially a method of manipulation, since it is not directed towards developing the abilities of men to choose, but rather — while maintaining an appearance of choice — towards their reduction. On the other hand, the direct influencing of the system of values, although it is far from being negligible in the development of a new way of life, his relatively narrow limits. One cannot implant the sort of values in people which are irrelevant to their everyday life, that is, values which have no importance in their everyday activity.

Therefore, in order to produce changes in the structure of needs we must in the first place change the sphere of human activity, while at the same time making sure that the emerging needs could be satisfied. Thus if the sort of social mechanism could be brought into being which really permits workers to have their say in and to exercise control over decisions concerning production and distribution, this would provide much greater incentives for increasing the general cultural level and for changing consumption in a corresponding direction, than any sort of propaganda, however intensive it may be, in favour of cultural values.

"Meaningful" consumption can come into being only together with a meaningful life. The socialist pattern of civilisation must therefore extend over every sphere of life, from production to consumption. This, of course, also means that the speed of this transformation is not high at all and that for some time to come we may have to be satisfied with half-solutions. But, even so, it is most important in our opinion to outline the prospects of development to ensure that the concrete practical solutions will take place within this determined direction, and that they shall not exercise an opposite effect.

10
Andras Hegedus

THE SELF-CRITICISM OF SOCIALIST SOCIETY: A REALITY AND A NECESSITY

"Thus, bourgeois economics only achieved understanding of feudal, ancient and oriental society once bourgeois society had begun to criticise itself. To the extent that bourgeois economics did not merely enact a mythologising identification with the past, its critique of previous society (i.e. of the feudal society it still had to combat directly) was analagous to the critique of idolatry undertaken by christianity, or the critique of catholicism undertaken by protestantism." (Marx)

The nature of the changes in European socialism

In hardly more than a decade and a half profound changes have taken place within almost every field of social life in the socialist countries of Europe, from the economic to the cultural. For all their diversity a common nucleus can be found in the new forms in which socialist development has expressed itself, forms which have already given rise to a lot of discussion and perhaps even more misunderstanding, and continue to do so. This nucleus which unites the often apparently highly contradictory new social phenomena is their deep-rooted cause, which can therefore also serve as the key to understanding the development of socialism now in progress.

The motive force and true function of the changes remain frankly incomprehensible unless we recognise and acknowledge the fact that the socialist societies of Europe have, if not simultaneously and to the same extent, nevertheless reached, or

161

else are on the point of reaching, that stage of maturity and perfection in the development of their social formations at which *internal analysis — "self-criticism" in Marx's words — has, in historical terms, become not only possible, but also necessary.*

The final outcome of this by no means complete social process will be to go once and for all beyond the situation in which "internal" indentification with socialism made it obligatory to defend the forms prevailing at any time against "external" criticism — criticism often backed up by force of arms. The time is already at hand when this position will become unambiguously apologetic and, as regards its objective function, not so much the expression of a commitment to the socialist path of social progress as of an obstinate defence of particular interests aiming to sustain forms already overtaken by the course of social development.

In order to be able to understand the current situation and recognise the changes outlined above as historically necessary, we must briefly review the initial phase of the socialist states' existence and the emergence of socialist property relations. The period in question saw the way towards any investigative analysis of this system forcibly barred after an extraordinarily short space of time. The problem facing us today is to overcome precisely this state of affairs.

The active negation of capitalism in the European socialist movements prior to the victory of the October Revolution in 1917 led necessarily to the belief that a society could and "must" be built which would create better and more human conditions than those of capitalism, conditions radically different in every respect from those of capitalism, and indeed, which would do so within a relatively short period of time.

Initially strengthened by the conviction that the victory of socialism would occur in the most developed countries and that it would not be confined to a single country, this belief was able to find support in scientific analysis of the then prevailing conditions. It did not, however, take into account the possibility that the ideals of a new society, the ideals of socialism, would triumph in a relatively backward part of the world and in one country alone. Even though this belief proved, at least for the time being, to be illusory (and it is primarily the historical reasons which I have given that account for the original conception of socialism), it cannot be denied that it did play a positive role by way of the notions of the new society that developed, for these reinforced the struggle of humanity for the creation of a new, more human order of society.

After 1917 the triumph of marxist-leninist ideas in Russia enabled these conceptions to come to grips in theoretical terms with a reality which could not yet, however, be fulfilled in practice.

After the new socio-economic conditions had been attained there arose — certainly not for the first time in history, nor even the last — a situation which rendered the real analysis of the new society, criticism of itself, impossible. In face of the "external" criticism which obstinately defended the old system, after the devastation of the war and in one of the poorest and most backward countries in Europe, conceptions of socialism to a large extent became ossified intrinsically, necessarily we might say, into dogmas regarded as indisputable articles of faith.

Any attempt to tear down this web of illusions about the new society, even in matters of secondary importance, seemed in the first phase of realising the triumphant new relations a deadly threat, irrespective of the subjective intentions; this reaction was usually not without foundation in so far as the *actual functioning* of such attempts was concerned. A historical situation arose in the infancy of the Soviet Union, and to a certain extent in the European peoples' democracies too in the early stages of their existence, in which any objectivity would have been bound to undermine the willingness to accept sacrifices in the struggle against the old system, or at least appear to do so, and objectivity had therefore to be seen as "veiled" counter-revolution. And so, after the triumph of the new relations, the shout of "Crucify him!" necessarily went up not only against those who had directly or indirectly come into conflict with the revolutionary transformation, but also against those who demanded more discriminating consideration of the facts, real analysis of the newly arisen social conditions.

Lenin at this time put into words one of the fundamental

choices of the epoch: "Every individual must place himself either upon our side or else upon the other. Anyone who attempts to sit on the fence will fail lamentably." This dichotomy, real in Lenin's day, later became an abnormal limitation upon individuals' freedom of choice, and hence played a significant role in the emergence of the social phenomenon now usually referred to as the "error of the personality cult". But at the time it corresponded exactly to the historical situation, for the basic problem for the social forces moulding historical events after the revolution was indeed either to maintain power or to be obliged to surrender it; beside this, every other question regarding the optimisation and humanisation of the new system paled into insignificance. This situation did not only create the curious dilemma as to whether the immediate task was to reinforce centralism and the rapidly developing administration or else extend democratic rights, it also determined the decision made on this count. Symbolised by the Kronstadt rebellion, the dilemma took on its most acute and perhaps also its most tragic aspect at the Tenth Congress of the CPSU, at a time in which the question as to how to proceed was still open: it was partly as a result of the Soviet leadership's experiences with a revolt of sailors misled by the anarchists that they were compelled to restrict democratic rights. Although, at Lenin's suggestion, the temporary character of these measures was emphasised, they later became a provision regarded as continuing to be applicable for a long time to come.

In this respect there arose relatively quickly the "ideal type" of socialism in which, particularly from the early 1930s onwards, the formal elements progressively became dominant over the material moments. This process was further accelerated by Lenin's death. The institutions and methods of leadership resulting from the complex web of the historical conditions became ossified for a period of decades, and became incontestable in law. Out of all this logically emerged the system of planning directives, the system of individual performance based on work-norms, socialist realism, and reverence for the leader in his position of sole responsibility — phenomena which were all declared essential to the welfare of society. And with the exception of Yugoslavia, all the European peoples' democracies which were engaged on the path of socialist development took this over as a ready-made model.

Of course, it soon became apparent that the institutional forms which arose after the victory of socialism were very different from the conceptions which arise as projections into the future during the struggles for the victory of socialism. The courageous attempt to correct conceptions which had proved illusory, an attempt which Lenin can be seen to have made after 1917, faded in the concrete historical situation. Yet in the initial phase, as I would emphasise repeatedly, all this had a real *raison d'être* in serving to defend the system, and this process, at least in this context and up to a certain point in time, can hardly be seen as anything other than the historically necessary form of the defence of the new social relations under extraordinarily difficult conditions.

The changing role of illusions about socialism

It was not the first time in history that the process described above had developed. When new socio-economic formations appear on the stage of history for the first time, they sustain for a long time those conceptions of the "new order" which formed before victory, during the struggle for its realisation, and this rigidifies their conceptions into mere dogmas. When confronted with practice, however, part of these ideas necessarily proves to be illusory, since no revolutionary movement has ever arisen which did not conceive the order it was fighting to bring about as constituting a better, finer, more human world than reality permitted. Things will in all probability be no different in the future, even if the role of the conscious element increases considerably and hence also the possibility of a more exact forecast. Can any but those "wise after the event" take it upon themselves today to contest the progressive role of the illusions which arose in the struggles waged by the socialist-communist movements to open up a new road for social development and consolidate the victorious new order? It was not least these illusions which sustained the often superhuman self-sacrifice necessary for victory and for the consolidation of the new order, a self-sacrifice whose fruits could often be enjoyed only by those who came afterwards.

But history often sees the consolidation of a new order followed relatively quickly by a tragic reversal of roles. The illusions no longer relate to the future, to the order which the participants are seeking to attain, but to one that has already been realised. Therefore, they now begin to fulfil a fundamentally different function, and cease after a certain period of time to support any vigorous involvement in the struggle for progress; they no longer contribute to the consolidation of the new order, but serve as often very primitive apologetics on behalf of the rigidified institutionalised forms of the prevailing conditions, apologetics which increasingly impede social development. The illusions about the new order can play a positive role even after the "victory" of the latter; it is a period in which they still assist in the consolidation of the triumphant "new order". But sooner or later, this period necessarily comes to a close. As the new order is consolidated, this attitude becomes increasingly reactionary and impedes progress more and more, for the time has meanwhile been approaching in which the confrontation of the illusions with reality, that is to say the "internal analysis" of the new socio-economic formation, becomes a reality and at the same time a historical necessity. On this basis, the new demands which have matured in the course of development must be formulated and the struggle to realise them taken up. This struggle will in its turn be affected by illusions about the possibilities of development in different respects, but such illusions will now be directed towards the future once more, and no longer towards what has already been realised.

But the transformation of the progressive role of the old illusions into an impediment to progress — a tragic change of role which often occurs within the lifetime of a single generation — cannot proceed until the young Hercules grows stronger, for illusion, like the whistling of the lone wayfarer in a dark wood, increases strength and plays a progressive role, even though this strength cannot yet be exercised in the practice of everyday life. Yet the destiny of a child is to grow up: one day he will come to a stage at which, as an adult, he will only be able to maintain the world of his former conception at the cost of childish behaviour and infantile attitudes, a stage at which everyday needs and experiences will force his old conceptions to confront reality.

Even in the lives of individuals this process is accompanied by difficulties, for the reality of the adult is on the whole poorer and more barren than the world conceived by the child. This phase is all the more difficult in the life of peoples and nations, where the "loss of illusions" and the development of real self-knowledge on the part of society is mostly achieved through arduous social struggles. For immediately after the victory of the new order, social groups form with an interest either in maintaining illusions about the real state of society or with an interest in overcoming these illusions.

This change could only be inscribed upon the historical agenda as a real and necessary task once socialism had consolidated itself against both internal and external opposition, when the choice between taking power or surrendering it had given way to the extremely complex and contradictory task of optimising and humanising the new system. For this to happen, the consolidation of the relations had to be so far advanced that any effort to re-establish the old relations had become chimerical, that the way back to a society based on capitalist private property was cut off and the return of factories, banks and landed property to the original owners (and thus the restoration of a new capitalist class, however constituted) made impossible in practical terms. When this is the case, when reactionary social initiatives have lost their breeding-ground and represent nothing more than the blind creed of tiny sects, only then can a critical relation develop towards the prevailing forms from the standpoint of the new dilemma now historically mature, from the standpoint of optimising and humanising society: in other words, criticism rooted in the "new order".

In addition, one condition must be present that is of great practical importance for the consolidation of the new order, namely that stabilisation takes place on the basis of the new socio-economic formation. So long as this condition is not fulfilled, any objective analysis takes on the appearance of being personally motivated and of its true objective being achieved not in the development of social relations but in gaining some change for the individual. In the early stages the aim of securing the positions of particular individuals fused with the defence of the given forms; and the latter seemed directly identical with the interests of social development. As a result of this dual aspect of false identification, any effort at real analysis of the given forms encountered extraordinarily strong resistance, even when it was conscious of being entirely committed to the cause of socialism. The social sciences registered this reaction in particularly marked fashion, probably being — or at least claiming to be — best equipped to find an answer to the real problems of social development.

Th dilemma of the social sciences: analysis or manipulation?

During the initial period of the socialist societies' development, the factors we have sketched out above led to a single function being ascribed to those sciences which examine the problems of our time; this function was propaganda on behalf of the prevailing political practice, the "legally sanctioned" forms. Anyone offending against this rule drew upon himself the accusation of being a reactionary and a defender of the bourgeoisie. In a historical conjuncture of this kind any scientific "objectivity", even when wholeheartedly committed to social progress, seemed a hostile element to be proceeded against with all the rigour of the law for the sake of defending socialism.

In this situation marxism — and in a narrower sense, marxist social science in particular — soon found itself in an apparently hopeless position. Its development temporarily came to a halt, many of its theses rigidified into dogmas, and it was tricked out with mystically developed, seemingly absolute ideological arguments. (Isolated and largely mystified slogans understandably proved better adapted to defending the established forms than did the creative new facts of social development or the new findings of other scientific currents relating to marxist social science.)

This explains why it was above all in the context of ideological life and marxist social science that the social changes described above made their mark; in fact one often gets the impression that marxism, consolidated into dogmas, was in the forefront of putting ideological obstacles in the way of innovation.

But here too we must avoid merely grasping phenomena superficially and considering them in ahistorical terms. In the Soviet Union of the 1920s and even the 1930s marxism, as an ideology that had become determinant, played an extremely important and basically positive role in the defence of socialism and the development of central administration. This social function simultaneously transformed marxist ideology, and even marxism itself, so as to accord with its particular requirements, and in two respects especially gave rise to serious deformation of it. It impeded the confrontation between (a) ideology and the development of the sciences, and between (b) ideology and social reality, and during certain periods rendered any such confrontation impossible.

There could, however, be no greater error than to attempt to grasp this state of affairs as a subjective error to be laid at the door of particular individuals; nor would superior scientific logic be on the side of an explanation which attributed it to the typical characteristics of the socialist social system: both interpretations fail to analyse social development in historical terms. The development in the socialist countries of a creative marxism conforming both to *scientific* insight and *social reality* has an objective base just as much as the deformed marxism which, as described above, shuts itself off from scientific findings and the facts of everyday reality. Now that the interests of social development require it, the new qualities of marxism are breaking through in spite of the subjective wishes and particular interests of individuals.

One of the most striking and characteristic signs of the self-analysis of socialist conditions is to be found in the socialist countries of Europe, in the appearance of a "social science" which is concerned with "today" and with the "official" recognition of its real social function. This has marked the end of the period in which literature seemed to be the only force capable of bringing real problems on to the "stage" of society in the face of the prevailing illusions. In this respect a significant role has in recent decades been played by sociology, which has increasingly developed in the socialist countries; this discipline has given rise to much discussion in the past, and will surely again do so in the future. Sociology, together with the other sciences dealing with contemporary problems, began to play a role in scientific life, to claim its citizenship, so to speak, during that period of the European socialist countries' development in which these new socio-economic systems saw the analysis of their own conditions become a social reality.

It is only in this context that the discussions stimulated in the socialist countries by those social sciences which deal with contemporary questions (including sociology) can correctly be assessed. As the whole previous development of sociology confirms, this science seems on the one hand to be the product of self-criticism on the part of socialism, and on the other hand that branch of the social sciences which represents society's most direct scientific instrument for acquiring knowledge of itself and for subjecting the social conditions to real analysis. Thus it is both the product of the new phase of the European socialist countries' development and at the same time the instrument which pushes development further. Also attributable to the changes under discussion is what has become generally recognised as the basic problem of marxist sociology in the socialist countries today: is it the job of this newly reborn and already fashionable science to provide information and data for the defence of the established forms (manipulation), or to help overcome these forms by analysing them critically (the analytic function)?

In the struggle of contradictory social forces, this dichotomy often seems an obscure, insoluble, dilemma, as if the sociologist or social scientist who deals with contemporary problems were compelled to choose between the two sides and could not undertake both functions simultaneously. The extent to which self-analysis on the part of the European socialist countries has matured as a historical reality and necessity makes it unnecessary for science to be fixated on such paralysing choices; even today perspectives of this kind can unambiguously be consigned to the sphere of false dilemmas.

The new economic reform: the product and the test of the
"self-analysis" of socialism

The significance of this phase of development from the point of view of the future of socialism can hardly be overstated, for it has resulted not only in a dynamisation of scientific and intellectual life (an effect it continues to have) but also in the moulding of the social conditions, in many varied respects. It is currently the determining factor of the new historical developments in the socialist countries; without it, for example, the kind of penetrating reform of the socialist economic system that has been carried through in Czechoslovakia and Hungary could have been put on the agenda.

The "economic reforms" which arose as a consequence of the "internal analysis" made by the European socialist societies have set in motion processes whose development will enable the system to adapt to changing conditions, that is to say (to borrow an expression from cybernetics) it is becoming more "ultra-stable", and can thus accomplish a more dynamic and many-sided development than at present.

It is obvious that planned reform of the economic system is inseparable from the self-criticism of socialism. For example, the course which was adopted in Hungary subjected to criticism, or at the very least set a question-mark against, a whole series of forms of organisation and control which in the previous period had had the full sanction of law. The limelight of internal critical analysis has clarified problems as important as the system of planning directives (which has now been dissolved in favour of indirect methods of control-prices, credit, etc.), the bureaucratic determination of prices (now gradually being replaced by economic pricing), and the maximum concentration of industry (now to be superseded by efforts to find the optimum size for factories) and so on. By the old standards the New Economic System seems a terribly daring, wilful and senseless revolt against (what were believed to be) eternal laws; but in reality it is nothing but the "internal analysis" of socialism, with the ripening needs of society being recognised and their consequences acted upon. This is how we must judge these phenomena from the historical perspective, even if the elaboration of the model of the economic reform and its execution by those in authority demanded, and still demand, much personal courage, true commitment to social progress and disregard of particular interests.

The elaboration of the model of the New Economic System (I refer principally to the Hungarian formula, as the one I am best acquainted with) is of importance not only because it is based on scientific analyses which challenge the forms that were formerly considered "protected", but also because it has synthesised the findings of these analyses with the framework of the economic sub-system of society, and has thus very largely set a course of action and development in terms of goals and social standards. What makes this worth emphasising is that internal analysis or "self-criticism" on the part of socialism is, as can easily be demonstrated, only able to exercise a really decisive effect upon social development when it does not remain at the level of partial analysis and partial proposals but stimulates more far-reaching, comprehensive conceptions. And what development could be more natural and at the same time more desirable than one in which the reform of the economic system, based on the internal analysis of socialism, is followed by further, more all-embracing social reforms covering increasingly wide areas of social life, including the political and cultural system?

This change naturally proceeds amid constantly renewed social conflict, for an attempt to overcome an existing set of conditions causes a clash between the defenders of the old form and the advocates of the new. Such antagonism, however, will probably be less and less expressed on the national plane after the reforms envisaged in the economic reform have been realised, but will rather be restricted in most cases to particular factories, local government organs or other institutions. This change thus deserves our attention, for it enables self-analysis by the system to become an increasingly integral component of the activity of society's central directive institutions and organisations: the particular interests impeding this process will be less liable to become polarised, the defence of the existing institutional forms will gradually give way to efforts to help the essential aspects of socialist development prevail.

Some misunderstandings: the hopes and fears attached to "liberalisation"

The prospects for development show that what I have been writing about refers to the start of something new rather than some finished period; hence the incomprehension of many people in both the progressive and the reactionary camps — especially in the West — in the face of the events in the European socialist countries over the last fifteen years or so. With surprise and violently conflicting feelings they have watched this process produce analysis, uncontaminated by dogmatic or ideological conceptions and prejudices, of the institutions that arose after the victory of the socialist revolution and then remained ossified for decades, and of the prevailing forms of social organisation in general, analysis which has been accompanied by earnest efforts to adapt social conditions to the times in every respect. This confused undergrowth of misunderstandings can be seen in the way foreign voices responded to the basically positive development in internal Hungarian politics after 1956. If the scope of this article permitted, it would be useful to give an appropriate selection of these foreign reactions at this juncture.

Many people have interpreted the appearance of the "new" period in the light of their own particular interests, and have attempted to make an instrument for the furtherance of their own ends out of the self-analysis and "self-criticism" of socialism and the corollary obsolescence of the coercive, historically conditioned perspective mentioned above, which maintained that the cause of socialism was identical with the social forms arising within socialism. "Liberalisation" became the peculiar term pertaining to this misconception. The avowed opponents of social progress considered precisely that which demonstrated the maturity and vigour of socialism to be a proof of its weakness. Others at the same time attempted to use this concept to intimidate those who were pursuing a real internal analysis of the conditions out of commitment to the cause of socialism or who were subordinating their everyday activity to this goal. Those who put their hopes in liberalisation and those who feared it hysterically seemed between them to be building up a tragic common platform. It sometimes appeared that where these two forces met, a helpless spirit of innovation was caught in a vice, often seeming to be an involuntary plaything in the clash of powerful forces. We can now state with assured and hopefully not exaggerated optimism that in this respect more mature conditions already obtain, and that the changes which a few years ago where apparent only in embryonic form have now developed into a strong shoot.

Yet if we are not to become the victims of our own illusions, or of the pessimism which often takes hold when they have been dispelled, we must realise that "self-criticism" on the part of the new system is neither some sort of "revolt of the intellectuals" nor a "disturbance" induced by reactionary circles from outside, but a historical necessity serving social progress. Today the elementary interest of the European socialist societies demands that this process, which is now historically opportune, should become effective and be carried through to its conclusion. Progressive intellectuals can help in the formulation of the wishes and interests of the "masses", but they cannot become independent of them. If they sought to do so, all their efforts would be doomed to failure.

Of course, there could be no greater error than to believe that foreign and reactionary circles, the avowed enemies of social progress, will stand by and watch the appearance of the "internal" criticism of European socialism passively. But in my view, the principal difficulty here in central Europe will no longer derive from the activity of implacable reactionaries, but from the misconceptions over these questions (i.e. over the perspectives for the development of European socialism) reigning among those subjectively committed to the cause of social progress, misconceptions which will largely be backed up by particular interests. This underlines how important it is today for the theory of "mature" socialism based on the "internal analysis" of European socialism to develop faster. This refers both to the acceleration of the tempo of socio-economic development (optimisation) and on the closer adjustment of social conditions to human needs (humanisation).

I have attempted to demonstrate that "self-criticism" on the part of European socialism is a process arising from the inner

174

motive forces of the socio-economic formation, and that, at least in this part of the world, it is historically necessary to carry it further. But there could be no greater error than to assume that this whole question is confined to the European socialist countries. It would probably not be far wrong to say that this issue will become the key question of universal human progress in our time, for it is certainly necessary to clarify problems of the recent past in order to elaborate the course of future development.

The slowness and "difficult birth" of the process whereby European socialism's "internal analysis" has become a reality is primarily explained by two circumstances: the fact that this new socio-economic formation first appeared on the stage of history in the Soviet Union and was consolidated within a hostile environment; and the fact that the new conditions were secured, not only in the case of the Soviet Union but elsewhere too, in countries where the productive forces stood at a much lower level than in the developed capitalist countries. From this it follows that the socio-economic formations which will necessarily arise in the future and dissolve the social order based on private property in countries with developed productive forces will not have to follow such a violent course, since neither of the two historical factors outlined above will arise as a historically determining force. Thus the internal analysis of European socialism will also enable the "Western" forces of social progress to find favourable forms with which to overcome capitalism. Many initiatives towards creative work of this kind and the development of corresponding political activity are appearing, particularly in the Communist Parties of Italy and France.

The internal analysis of European socialism helps both the idea and the practice of socialism to exercise a revolutionising effect, not only in its prevailing, often accidental forms, but also because such analysis has made it possible for socialism to reveal its own essential aspects.

INDEX

Some other titles in the MOTIVE series

Michel Raptis
Revolution and Counter-Revolution in Chile

Henri Lefebvre
The Survival of Capitalism

Franz Jakubowski
Ideology and Superstructure in Historical Materialism

Agnes Heller
The Theory of Need in Marx

Jiri Pelikan
Socialist Opposition in Eastern Europe

Mihaly Vajda
Fascism as a Mass Movement

Hilda Scott
Women and Socialism—Experiences from Eastern Europe

Andras Hegedus
Socialism and Bureaucracy

Bill Lomax
Hungary 1956

Henri Laborit
Decoding the Human Message

Simon Leys
The Chairman's New Clothes—Mao and the Cultural Revolution